The Outcome Economy

The Outcome Economy

How the Industrial Internet of Things is Transforming Every Business

Joseph Barkai

Table of Contents

Foreword

Great change requires great vision that can glimpse into the future and offer a reason to leave the comfort of the past behind. This book is the roadmap with which we can begin to see, understand, and navigate that future.

During the past five decades, the world has undergone numerous transformations, from the Industrial Revolution, to electrification, to the Information Age we currently inhabit. Today we are at the threshold of yet another revolution, one that is likely to eclipse anything humanity has experienced to date—a revolution of hyper-connectivity where billions, and soon trillions, of devices are being woven into the fiber of every human experience, binding us together in unimagined ways and creating a culture of constant innovation. And yet, we are still in the earliest stages of global connectivity—stumbling our way through what it means to our organizations, our society, and ourselves as we find new ways to create value and meaning from this new normal.

As with any monumental shift in technology, the ultimate value cannot be guessed at or adequately predicted in advance of the behaviors that will evolve in its wake. These are behaviors that are deeply rooted in the past and which we are always reluctant to modify until we can no longer withstand the pain of the present or are drawn forward by the overwhelming value of the future.

Imagine that I've somehow rolled the clock back to the dawn of computing in the early 1960s and I told you that by 2020 there would be close to 100 billion connected computing devices. What would you have thought at that point in time? Most likely that I was being absurd! How could we possibly use that many devices? Who would build them? How could they be affordable? Why would we even need a small fraction of that many devices? When Motorola introduced the first cell phone, which was affectionately called "the brick," pundits projected fewer than ten million cell phones by the turn of the century. Yet, today, there are more than 7 billion cell phones, of which 2 billion are smart phones. As the economist Paul Romer has said, "… every generation has underestimated the potential for finding new … ideas … possibilities do not merely add up; they multiply."

It is this multiplication effect that is most elusive in projecting the trajectory of the future. New technology creates new behaviors, which create new sources of economic value. That value, in turn, creates greater demand for new technology. And the accelerator that causes this cycle to turn from a spark into a blaze is not the connections, or the devices, or the networks, but rather the fundamental change in how we create value.

That is the essence of this book; it looks well beyond the simple concept of connectivity to delve into the specific ways in which new value is being created and how that will alter the most basic economics of how we live, work, and play. It offers a concrete understanding of how the Internet of Things is transforming business models by taking the quantum leap from companies that make promises about products, to companies that promise outcomes to a collaborative and interconnected world in which success hinges on how well you can integrate your organization as part of a complex ecosystem that will align itself around outcomes and innovation.

That may sound trivial, but it is likely to have even greater economic consequences than the shift from the craftsmen and artisans of the 16th and 17th centuries, to the Industrial Revolution and mass production of the 19th and 20th centuries; call it mass innovation on a scale that we've never thought possible.

In this hyperconnected world, nothing is too ambitious. The greatest problems that we face, not only as organizations but as a civilization, will be far less daunting because of the ability to deliver outcomes that marshal vast global networks of talent, resources, and data. For the first time in history, we will soon be able to understand how people, machines, and systems behave on a global scale, across all boundaries, known and unknown.

Farfetched? No more so than any other great change has been. Our limitations in imagining the future are only those that we impose on our imagination. This book will change what you can imagine, and in doing so it will change how you chart your own course into the future.

Thomas Koulopoulos
Chairman, Delphi Group
Boston, MA
April 2016

Preface:
Why This Book?

The digital age and the era of the Internet of Things (IoT) are upon us. We are bombarded by a nonstop onslaught of attention-grabbing headlines about a brave new world in which connected, chatty toasters and refrigerators in "smart homes" are communicating with each other, presumably to better our lives.

And the same is going on in the industrial realm. The Industrial Internet of Things, frequently dubbed Industry 4.0, promises a world of connected robots and remotely operated machinery that, when strung together, deliver greater manufacturing productivity, better products, and reduced ecological impact.

There are plenty of compelling arguments—albeit not satisfactory commercial evidence (at least not yet)—that the Internet of Things is one of the most important transformative differentiators we've seen in decades, perhaps even in a century.

But the sheer volume of noise, buzzwords, and tired clichés that serve to amplify promises from rosy-glasses-donning vendors make it hard to sort out the real from the hype and the possible from the red herrings. It is increasingly difficult to gain clarity about the actual business value of many of these new ideas and the long-term impact they will have on manufacturing companies, the workplace, and society at large.

All too often, it's challenging to articulate the context of specific business problems, i.e., how to discover and realize the opportunities that will benefit *your* business and *your* customers.

In this book, I wanted to look beyond the mere concept of device connectivity to offer a concrete understanding of how the Internet of Things is transforming business models in specific and tangible ways that are creating new value in practically every business and every workplace.

Just as importantly, I wanted to avoid some of the overplayed technology topics in the Internet of Things discourse, such as communication technologies, data security and privacy, and the hyperbole about how many devices are going to be connected to the Internet in the future. While certainly interesting and extremely important, these topics can be dangerously distracting and lead us astray from what must be at the core of the Industrial Internet of Things narrative: the fundamental change in the ways in which we are going to create value in the future.

This perspective may not always be in agreement with the mainstream attention-grabbing point of view you often encounter, but I hope it will offer alternative thinking to help you chart the path of *your* Industrial Internet of Things strategy.

Joe Barkai
Needham, MA
May 2016

Acknowledgements

Many individuals mentioned in the book, and some that aren't, have dedicated time to speak with me about the Industrial Internet of Things. I would like to thank them for sharing their experiences, aspirations, and visions about the connected world.

I would also like to thank Tom Koulopoulos for his astute insight and invaluable advice.

Finally, I must recognize the many clients and colleagues from whom I continue to learn every day.

1

Welcome to the Outcome Economy

If everybody minded their own business the world would go round a deal faster than it does.

—THE DUCHESS

The Spanish national railway company Renfe[1] operates 26 high-speed trains on the Barcelona-Madrid-Malaga line.

Renfe is committed to delivering exceptional on-time service to its customers. In fact, Renfe offers a unique money-back guarantee that reimburses passengers on the Alta Velocidad

Española (AVE) train for the full ticket price if a train is late by more than 15 minutes.

To ensure that it can deliver that level of service commitment to passengers, Renfe has contracted the maintenance of the trains and tracks to the train manufacturer Siemens AG. Siemens' maintenance operations monitor and analyze data from hundreds of sensors on the trains and tracks to detect malfunctions that could cause service disruptions, and schedules the necessary remedial maintenance work in advance of any impending critical failure.

Since the system was put into operation, only one in 2,300 trains didn't meet the guaranteed uptime requirement, which equates to service availability of 99.94 percent!

And commuters took notice. Before the guaranteed performance model was put in place, 80 percent of passenger traffic between Madrid and Barcelona was by air. In 2008, with the system in operation, 60 percent of all passengers along this route opted to take the AVE train instead of flying.

What had Renfe done? What makes this program different from other, more conventional passenger service contracts? Renfe created a business model in which the value paid and value received are tied directly to *outcomes most meaningful to passengers.*

Welcome to the "outcome economy," where companies create value not just by selling products and services, but by delivering complete solutions that produce *meaningful quantifiable business outcomes* for customers. Stated differently, customers in the outcome economy are not looking to just buy products; they want to buy a *guarantee of an outcome*.

What, exactly, is a business outcome? For many years, business theorists and marketing gurus have sought to understand what customers truly want and how to define, deliver and measure that elusive "customer value." Harvard Business School marketing professor Theodore Levitt[2] famously framed the problem succinctly:

> *People don't want to buy a quarter-inch drill.*
> *They want a quarter-inch hole!*

Business outcomes are measured by the business goals the product makes possible. Rather than using technical specifications and bureaucratic transactional terms to define a product, such as horsepower, maintenance response times and hours billed, a set contract value, or even total cost of ownership, an outcome is measured based on its ability to meet business-centered performance criteria.

Rolls-Royce's TotalCare service[3] has become the poster child of outcome-based service.

TotalCare is a suite of maintenance and repair services for the company's commercial jet engines that includes continuous monitoring of engine health parameters. As the product/service provider, Rolls-Royce assumes the responsibility for "time-on-wing" (that's the term the aviation industry uses to describe how much time an engine is available) and maintenance costs. Rolls-Royce's customers—the airlines—do not buy jet engines; they pay for engine time-on-wing availability or, you might even say, they pay for lift power. And they do not pay Rolls-Royce unless the engine under contract actually delivers it.

When viewed from an airline's business point of view, TotalCare service significantly reduces capital expenditure because it no longer owns the engines. The airline experiences fewer disruptions and more satisfied travelers because of the tight service-level agreement with Rolls-Royce. Additionally, maintenance operation costs and spare parts inventory are streamlined, as most of these activities are now being outsourced.

Surrendering profits from direct jet engine sales doesn't mean Rolls-Royce is at the losing end of the new business arrangement with the airlines. Traditionally, Rolls-Royce expected additional 5 percent incremental revenue from engine sales. But as engines impact about 70 percent of the operational costs for the airline, and with 13,000 commercial jet engines in service, Rolls-Royce has built an outcome-based business that delivers predictable recurring revenues and a competitive advantage. TotalCare service is a strong brand booster.

In the long run, the outcome economy will rid many companies from having to own and operate assets (factories, equipment, and people) in order to generate value. More companies will orchestrate, share, and sell value using excess capacity of assets, services, and people that are owned (or partially owned) by others. We are already seeing the harbingers and early adopters of this phenomenon in several non-manufacturing sectors such as Uber, Zipcar, Airbnb, and numerous others.

The notion that customers want outcomes, such as drilled holes and lift power, and care much less about owning and operating the physical asset that produces those outcomes, may be intuitively obvious. But for most companies, this is a challenging prospect, as they will be compelled to develop and cultivate a deeper understanding of their customers' businesses, know how their products and services are being used, and learn how customers measure and evaluate business and product outcomes.

Product and service owners need a means to measure business outcomes on an ongoing basis, often in real time. Service providers need to be able to sense when a promised outcome isn't being delivered and take the necessary remedial action or else be penalized by their customer.

Achieving a Competitive Advantage

The outcome economy represents a radical shift in how product and services companies compete.

Product differentiation and market competition in the traditional product-centric economy are driven by product features and cost, and, in some cases, by offering extended warranties and service contracts. When designing and selling a piece of equipment in this product-centric economy, all you need to do is demonstrate that the product adheres to published specifications and provide adequate warranty service coverage.

Product-centric business paradigm is based on reducing manufacturing costs to increase unit volume sales and, at the same time, incorporate built-in obsolescence to protect against market saturation.

By contrast, in the outcome economy, physical products don't count as much as the business outcome they deliver to your customers. You must guarantee future product outcome (for example, uptime) and future business outcome (such as air traveler throughput).

The new model is one in which products "pull through" profitable services that offer predictable recurring revenue for a long time after they are sold.

To survive and thrive in the new economy, companies will have no choice but to have better data and analytic tools to measure performance, calculate costs, and manage the risks associated with guaranteeing business outcomes. Better data analytics capabilities will also bring new pricing practices based on the opportunity probability and calculated risk of delivering outcomes.

The outcome economy is upon us. The question now is a simple one: is your business ready?

Chapter Takeaways

- The outcome economy: "People don't want to buy a quarter-inch drill. They want a quarter-inch hole." –Theodore Levitt

- Companies in the outcome economy shift from competing through selling products and services, to competing by delivering a guarantee for measurable results that are important to the customer.

- Products in the outcome economy "pull through" profitable services that offer predictable recurring revenue for a long time after they are sold.

- To survive and thrive in the new economy, companies must develop a deeper understanding of their customers and their customers' business.

- Better data and analytic tools to measure performance, calculate costs, and manage risks associated with guaranteeing business outcomes are critical to success in the outcome economy.

2

The Fourth
Industrial Wave

*"Begin at the beginning and go on till
you come to the end; then stop."*
—THE KING OF HEARTS

We often chronicle the history of industrialization in the Western Hemisphere as a series of "industrial revolutions." The First Industrial Revolution began in Britain in the late 18th century with the mechanization of the textile industry; manual tasks previously performed laboriously by dozens of individual weavers in their homes were transformed and consolidated into large cotton mills, employing thousands of workers. The modern factory, characterized by centralization of operations and machine automation, was born.

The Second Industrial Revolution came about a hundred years later, in the early 20th century. The introduction of the electrically powered conveyor belt and Frederick Taylor's continuous-flow production methods led to the famous Ford moving assembly line. The era of mass production had arrived.

The first two industrial revolutions had a profound effect on the economy and society, an impact that was to last nearly 100 years.

The newly built factories created strong demand for additional cheap labor and new skills, allowing more women to be a growing part in the industrial workforce, but, at the same time, this was also the beginning of wage discrimination that persists today.

The Second Industrial Revolution and mass production made many luxury items more affordable and within reach for average people. It added job opportunities and accelerated urban development that led to the formation of the middle class.

But these industrial revolutions also had a devastating effect on many skilled laborers that had lost their jobs to steam- and electrically-powered machines. People who lost their source of income in the country had no choice but to move to the cities and usually ended up working in the same factories that took away their livelihood.

Working conditions in the majority of factories were horrendous. Factory owners used cheap, unskilled workers to lower the cost of production, frequently using child and underpaid labor.

The third wave of industrial innovation and economic disruption, also referred to as the Digital Revolution, was set off by advances in computing, information, and communication technology (ICT) in the late 20th century. It was typified by the gradual change from analog mechanical and electrical automation to digital technology—a process that began around the middle of the 20th century with the invention of the transistor.

I chose to use the term ICT (Information and Communication Technology) as it covers all forms of that IT (Information Technology) covers, with an extra focus on all forms of communication.

Massive investments in research and development, and application of digital technologies in the 1950s and 1960s by the military and governments, pushed the technology forward, funding innovation, accelerating technology adoption, and driving costs down. In the 1980s and 1990s, the digital transformation reached consumers' homes through broadband and satellite communication—a momentum that continues relentlessly to the present day.

It's probably accurate to think of the Digital Revolution as a wave rather than a revolution. Digital technology has become a platform that propels innovation and upon which future industrial revolutions will be built.

> Throughout the book, I use the term 'Internet of Things' and the acronym 'IoT' to mean the same. 'Industrial Internet of Things' and 'Industrial IoT' refer to the application of the Internet of Things in industrial and manufacturing settings.

Today, the Fourth Industrial Revolution is under way. And it promises to be bigger and more profound than the previous ones. The new Industrial Revolution is the Internet of Things.

The Internet of Things is the network of physical objects, or "things," embedded with electronics, software, sensors, and actuators that enable these objects to connect, collect, exchange, and act on data they share.

These *smart, connected devices* can be operated and controlled remotely across existing wired and wireless network infrastructure. Many useful (and even many more useless) applications that exploit connectivity among consumer devices, appliances, and other everyday objects are showing up in the marketplace at a growing rate.

In the manufacturing industry, we think in terms of the Industrial Internet of Things, or as Europeans like to call it, Industry 4.0, in reference to the Fourth Industrial Revolution.

Like the previous three industrial revolutions, the Internet of Things will be highly disruptive. In fact, by all indications, it is poised to have an even more profound impact, as Thomas Koulopoulos observes:[4]

> *"The Industrial Internet of Things will alter the nature of business in ways that will make the Industrial Revolution look like a speed bump on the road towards automation."*

But unlike previous technological disruptions, which were observed and understood only ex post facto, the Industrial Internet of Things is already being analyzed, predicted, and overhyped to the point that one might challenge our ability to look that far into the future and understand its social and economic impact.

Historical Perspective

As many are quick to observe, the Internet of Things isn't exactly a new phenomenon. Even before the dawn of the digital revolution, various forms of wired and wireless telemetry and remote monitoring were exploited for a variety of industrial and military applications, albeit using far less capable technologies than are available to us today. A brief recap of the history of the Internet of Things is both interesting and illustrative.

In the late 19th century, French engineers built a system of weather monitoring and snow-depth sensors that transmitted real-time weather information from Mont Blanc to Paris. In the 1930s, weather balloons (again, a French invention) transmitted temperature and pressure measurements, encoded in Morse code, wirelessly.

Fast forward to the Digital Revolution era. The aggressive growth in the public telephone infrastructure and the gradual introduction of digital communication over existing analog voice-grade telecommunication lines, paved the way to machine to machine (M2M) communication in a variety of defense, industrial and commercial applications. Perhaps most noteworthy are the concepts and patents developed in the 1970's by Theodore G. Paraskevakos,[5] which included a portable cardiac alarm system, an automatic utility meter reading, and digital vending machine communication.

In 1982, a modified Coca-Cola vending machine at Carnegie Mellon University became the first Internet-connected appliance, communicating beverage stock levels directly to dorm rooms.

> The origin of the term "Internet of Things," although recent, is unknown. Many believe it started at Procter & Gamble in 1999 during discussions of the applications of the then red-hot-topic of radio frequency identification (RFID) in P&G's supply chain operations.

Multiple technological advancements have led to, and continue to fuel, the accelerated rate of embedding control software in industrial and consumer products, and hyper-connecting smart devices that form the Internet of Things:

- Increase in computing power and the corresponding rapid decline in cost, power consumption, and physical footprint of computing devices and sensor technologies.
- Ubiquitous wireless communication that offers superior bandwidth, as costs continue to decline.
- Widespread adoption of Internet communication protocol with its extremely large address space that can accommodate as many unique IoT devices as needed.[6]
- Development and increased use of standard communication and security protocols that make connecting disparate devices from different vendors easier and better secured.
- Adoption of cloud computing technology[7] by large enterprises and the formation of Internet-based infrastructure that provides shared storage and processing resources on demand.

These advancements are driving an unprecedented wave of technology and business innovation in both consumer products and industrial equipment.

The Industrial Internet of Things

What, exactly, is the Industrial Internet of Things?

A reasonably good starting point can be found in Wikipedia:

> *The Internet of Things (IoT) is the network of physical objects—devices, vehicles, buildings and other items—embedded with electronics, software, sensors, and network connectivity that enables these objects to collect and exchange data. The IoT allows objects to be sensed and controlled remotely across existing network infrastructure, creating opportunities for more direct integration of the physical world into computer-based systems, and resulting in improved efficiency, accuracy and economic benefit; when IoT is augmented with sensors and actuators, the technology becomes an instance of the more general class of cyber-physical systems, which also encompasses technologies such as smart grids, smart homes, intelligent transportation and smart cities. Each thing is uniquely identifiable through its embedded computing system but is able to interoperate within the existing Internet infrastructure.*[8]

In the industrial manufacturing sector, machines and processes that used to operate in isolation are coming together to form a fully integrated, automated, and optimized production flow, leading to greater process efficiencies, reduced waste, enhanced output quality, and improved supply chain traceability and efficiency.

The Industrial Internet of Things is driving the Fourth Industrial Revolution. It is changing traditional production relationships among suppliers, producers, and customers— as well as between humans and machines— and promoting disruptive business transformation by redefining and reorganizing the product value chain as we previously understood it from the early days of vertical integration and unified flow were implemented at Henry Ford's factories in the early part of the 20th century.

And one of the most profound ways this is happening is through the melding of cyber and physical worlds.

Cyber-Physical Systems and the Digital Twin

It is becoming increasingly easier and cheaper to instrument a piece of equipment, add sensors and microchips, and to connect it to the Internet, forming an IoT device.

Industrial IoT-connected equipment can operate in two parallel worlds simultaneously: the physical system that performs its intended tasks and interacts with users and other systems, and a digital replica—a "digital twin"—of the same piece of equipment that resides somewhere within the corporate ICT infrastructure. The digital twin provides a mechanism to project physical objects into the digital world. It is a way to monitor the status and control the operation of the actual physical object through the digital model.

The digital twin isn't a mere software dashboard to view or change status remotely, nor is it a generic model of a general class of physical assets such as motors or pumps. Rather, each physical system (or subsystem) is represented by a unique digital instance that corresponds to the physical device and is specific to the features, attributes, and operational aspects of that piece of equipment that are critical to task performance and achieving the intended business outcome. For instance, the digital twin "knows" the exact configuration of a wind turbine, its current operating and power generation profile, its maintenance history, and similar information needed to operate and maintain it.

The digital twin "experiences" the physical product continually—in real time if necessary—and throughout its lifecycle. Utilizing the digital twin, product manufacturers and brand owners know much more about their products in the field than ever before. They know how well products perform; they understand how end-consumers are using these products and how effectively they operate and utilize them, and when products fail and why.

> The integration of physical objects and digital systems and the blurring of the boundaries between them is sometimes referred to as "Cyber-Physical Systems."

This rich, multifaceted information gives product companies invaluable insight that helps them mature their products more rapidly, fix faults more quickly, and do a better job tailoring products to individual business needs and user profiles.

An early example of the use of telemetry to improve product reliability and gain greater insight into customer experience is the use of General Motors OnStar system[9] that provides owners of GM automobiles with diagnostics, informs them when basic maintenance needs to be performed, and provides remote assistance that varies from roadside assistance to remotely unlocking your car's doors.

But GM also uses OnStar to identify problems on new vehicles before they go on sale and throughout the ownership experience. In an interview,[10] Jamie Hresko, previously GM's Vice President of Quality, said:

> *We can look at virtually thousands and thousands of performance metrics within the engine via OnStar. It gives us a huge strategic advantage.*

OnStar technology gives GM insight about the performance of engines now in production. But what about the myriad of other factors that might help design better and safer cars of the future? GM plans to pair OnStar-equipped cars with a Mobileye[11] advanced road-tracking camera and software to harvest crowed-sourced information about driving patterns and gather precision-mapping information to support future autonomous vehicles.

Manufacturing Goes Digital: The Factory of the Future

The new insights provided by cyber-physical systems are also changing some of the fundamentals of the manufacturing plant.

The factory of the past, which was formed during the highly transformative First and Second Industrial Revolutions, was based on cranking out identical products at the fastest rate possible. Henry Ford famously said that car buyers could have any color they liked as long as it was black; which, we think, wasn't intended to disrespect customers but rather to maximize the throughput and the utilization of his factory's equipment and labor. The efficiency principles developed by Henry Ford and Frederick Taylor continued to dictate manufacturing operations for over a century.

For decades, companies built factories in low-wage regions with a single focus: curtail labor costs. But many of the assumptions about markets and customer expectations, and the business models that reigned for over a century started to crumble in the latter part the last century.[12] Waves of globalization, low-cost competition, offshoring, and increasingly demanding customers—all are forcing product companies to rethink century-old product design and manufacturing strategies.

But with the advent of automation and process optimization techniques, labor costs are less significant, diminishing the need to offshore manufacturing. Product companies are now moving back to more wealthy countries not because wages in low-cost countries are rising, but because they need to be closer to their customers and orchestrate agile supply chains so that they can respond as fast as possible to changes in consumer preferences and manage demand fluctuations.

The factory of the future will focus on mass customization, i.e., making smaller batches of a wider variety of products, each tailored precisely to every customer's wishes, without forfeiting the benefits of global supply chains operations.

This radical transformation is enabled by massive digitization of manufacturing assets. Manufacturing lines are becoming heavily instrumented and connected, offering unprecedented visibility into manufacturing operations on a global basis.

You can think of the Industrial Internet of Things as a technology and strategy to unify individual manufacturing facilities into a single virtual manufacturing plant. This enables product companies to operate individual operations to satisfy local market needs, and, at the same time, leverage insights from multiple facilities to drive innovation, optimize operations, enhance quality, and leverage global talent pools.

Not only is the manufacturing line being instrumented, but the entire value chain is being digitized, which does not only transform the way goods are made, but also how they are sold and serviced. With the Industrial Internet of Things, manufacturing and supply chains are both nimble and efficient at the same time, realizing the motto of next generation manufacturing: "Build anywhere; sell and service anywhere." And, as we'll see in the next chapter, this ability to be nimble and customize the factory process extends to virtually every industry, from wine-making to industrial manufacturing.

Chapter Takeaways

- The Internet of Things is the network of physical objects embedded with electronics, software, sensors, and actuators that enable these objects to connect, collect, exchange, and act on data.

- The digital twin, or a cyber-physical system, is a way to project physical objects into the digital world and view the status and control the operation of the actual physical object.

- The digital twin "experiences" the physical product continually, providing information about product performance, how it is being used, and when it fails and why.

- Factories of the future will be fully digitized, connected, and located closer to target markets. This will allow transition from mass production to precise and targeted mass customization.

- The Industrial Internet of Things enables product companies to implement the goal of next generation manufacturing: "Build anywhere; sell and service anywhere."

3

Big Cranes and
Digital Vineyards

---

*Why, sometimes I've believed as many
as six impossible things before
breakfast.*

—THE RED QUEEN

If thinking about the Industrial Internet of Things conjures up images of humming factory robots, large power plants, and bustling assembly lines, let me take you on a short trip to the winemaking regions of Europe. I will give you a firsthand view of how the Industrial Internet of Things and value chain digitization is changing every business.

eVinyard[13] is a digital vineyard system created by Elmitel, a Slovenian IoT company, and used by small vineyard owners in Eastern Europe, Spain, and Bordeaux, France. Elmitel installs wireless sensor networks from Spanish IoT company Libelium[14] in vineyards to collect microclimate conditions such as ambient and soil temperature and humidity, wind, rainfall, and leaf wetness to help owners plan maintenance activities such as irrigation and spraying against vineyard pests and diseases and, at the same time, reduce unnecessary chemical exposure.

This is how eVinyard's founder, Matic Šerc, described to me the role of the Internet of Things in precision agriculture:

> *Development of new technologies, the need for economically efficient food production, and the urgent need to protect the environment are pushing innovation in precision agriculture. Even the very traditional wine industry is adopting precision agriculture technologies and methods that increase owners' knowledge about their vineyard, optimize production, and help grow crops more sustainability.*

Not far away, in Lugano, Switzerland, the Swiss company Dolphin Engineering, developed PreDiVine:[15] another cloud-based decision support system based on wireless sensor networks (also from wireless sensor maker Libelium), weather stations, and software algorithms to predict the spread of vineyards diseases.

Using historical data combined with a database of pests and diseases and forecast algorithms, the software assesses the risk of disease development and helps optimize spraying to achieve maximum impact and reduce damage to the environment.

In our conversation, Dolphin Engineering's CEO Mauro Prevostini emphasized the business outcome PreDiVine users experience:

> *Owners now know, in advance, which kind of disease will appear, where and by when. They have less need for in-field observations and spare a lot of time and resources. Furthermore, they minimize the environmental effect of over-spraying.*

From Vineyards to Cranes

Finnish company Konecranes[16] is a vastly different example of how an industrial product company leverages the power of the Internet of Things.

Konecranes manufactures and services a line of heavy-load cranes and lifting equipment used in factories, ports, and shipyards. These machines are fitted with sensors that track the operating cycle and loads of the equipment and detect early signs of wear and tear. The information is transmitted back to the support center over the Internet.

Konecranes uses this real-time visibility and advanced warning signals to provide superior service to its customers. Service technicians travel to worksites to perform routine maintenance work and minor repairs, vastly reducing the likelihood of unscheduled major repair work.

Juha Pankakoski, Chief Digital Officer at Konecranes, is all about the business value of information. During multiple conversations we had, he stressed the importance of information—both technical and customer data—to drive product differentiation and achieve competitive advantage:

> *Improved understanding of customer data and product fit for purpose provides true competitive advantage.*

But in a sentiment that may appear—at least on the surface—somewhat incongruent with the grand aspirations of mass-instrumentation advocates, he adds:

> *Everything can be digital. But should everything be digital?*

And Mr. Pankakoski concludes:

> *We focus on what provides product value: what we can leverage in a way that the customer sees value in and is willing to pay for.*

Products as a Service

Konecranes' comprehensive approach to product quality and service is a great example of how the Industrial Internet of Things brings about a spectrum of new business opportunities to deliver and monetize customer value.

Product companies can offer the traditional ownership model where the customer owns the product and benefits from enhanced service efficiencies, or they can offer a *product-as-a-service* model, in which the manufacturer retains ownership of the product and takes full responsibility for operating and servicing products for a fee. In return, the service provider delivers a guaranteed outcome and performance level, as Rolls-Royce does with its TotalCare service program, which I described earlier, in Chapter 1.

And Konecranes takes this concept a step further. It shares some of the operational data it collects from its machines—data that most product companies would consider strategic and confidential—with its customers. The simple argument is that if customers use the data to improve their operation and drive higher utilization of Konecranes' hardware, they will remain loyal customers and brand champions.

Describing Siemens AG's Internet of Things strategy, Dr. Horst Kayser, the company's Chief Strategy Officer made a clear distinction between physical products and the business outcomes they deliver:

> *You may see hardware [in our products], but what you actually buy today is performance that is enhanced and optimized digitally.*

This is the essence of the value that the Industrial Internet of Things delivers, not just connectivity, but new business models that allow for limitless opportunity to innovate and reinvigorate every business.

Chapter Takeaways

- The Industrial Internet of Things brings about a range of new business models for delivering and monetizing value harvested from connected devices.

- Not every system that can be digitized and connected to the Internet should be. Focus on business outcomes that represent clear customer value.

- The Internet of Things forms the foundation for a product-as-a-service model, in which customers do not own physical products but pay for guaranteed outcomes and performance levels.

- The full potential of a product-as-a-service model is achieved through a rich and diverse collaborative ecosystem of information and service providers.

- Product-as-a-service companies create additional value by sharing operational data they collect from their machines—data that most product companies would consider strategic—with its customers and service partners.

4

Beyond Connectivity: Searching for Value in the Internet of Things

---

Everything's got a moral, if only you can find it.

—THE DUCHESS

The mere mention of the term "Internet of Things" inevitably evokes a conversation about network connections. How many "things" will be connected to the Internet in the future? To where, exactly? And how soon will it happen? Indeed, it seems not a day goes by without being bombarded by breathless headlines predicting the magnitude and future economic impact of the Internet of Things. These market forecasts, even those from the same information source, often vary by several orders of magnitude, casting serious doubts on the ability of pundits and analysts alike to define, explain, and ascertain the "size" of the Internet of Things marketplace.

But, when it's all said and done, does the number of connected devices really matter? Why? And to whom?

Well, it certainly matters to companies that make and sell communication hardware, sensors, and data acquisition devices. It also matters to the wireless carriers that seek to monetize the telemetry data that flows through their Internet "pipes." But it hardly matters to the product companies and brand owners that are trying to decipher and explore the potential impact the Internet of Things will have on their business and on their customers' businesses.

Connectivity is becoming an innate facility of practically every product; it is an expected commodity. We are rapidly approaching a time where everything and everyone is essentially a stationary or a roaming Internet node in an omnipresent, always-connected cloud, creating a global network of people, devices, and machines. Most of us carry an Internet-connected mobile device (and many carry two or more of them). More cars, home appliances, and medical alert and well-being monitoring devices are becoming connected, exchanging data and responding to events.

Connectivity enables the value-crating functionality of a product to exist and be delivered outside the physical boundaries of the device itself. Cloud connectivity connects value chain functions within and outside the product manufacturer to form new product and service offerings.

But connectivity itself does not inherently create value, it only *enables value*—which is why connectivity should not be the main focus of the Industrial IoT discourse.

The Wisdom of Things

In his book, *The Wisdom of Crowds: Why the Many Are Smarter Than the Few and How Collective Wisdom Shapes Business, Economies, Societies and Nations,*[17] James Surowiecki argues that the aggregation of information can result in decisions that are better than any that could have been achieved by any individual in the group. The mere connectedness among people in the group enables (but, again, it doesn't create) a new value.

Likewise, in the Internet of Things, networked information facilitates the *"Wisdom of Things"*: the collective information emanating from multiple sources (sensors, measurement devices, and even humans) is combined to enable and empower the extraction of new, previously unattainable, business value.

However, whereas the wisdom of crowds is predicated on a group of (hopefully) smart individuals, the Internet of Things is based on connectivity among devices that aren't necessarily "smart"—they can be "dumb" devices that collect and transmit data that is subsequently used by other upstream devices or cloud-based and back-office applications that utilize those data.

Consider, for example, a simple temperature sensor that can be read remotely via a wired or wireless connection. Most of us will not consider such a device "smart." Yet, this lowly temperature sensor can control the operation of a $10,000 commercial heating, ventilation, and air-conditioning (HVAC) system. When multiple sensors and HVAC units are interconnected to form a building energy management system, we get a useful and valuable business system. And we might as well agree that this energy management system is sufficiently "smart."

You can think of the human brain as an analogy: on their own, individual neurons and synapses are simple devices that lack consciousness, but connected, they collectively form a superior decision-making organ.

In other words, the idea of the Wisdom of Things underscores the point that the business value of the Internet of Things does not begin and end by enabling connectivity, and that the aggregated value of different sources is discoverable and useable not at the device level but rather away from it, in a remote part of the IoT network. This is a critical point that is often lost in the hyperbole about the *number* of connected things.

(You can refer to Appendix I: *Taxonomy of "Smart, Connected Things"* at the end of the book for a detailed discussion on this topic.)

Conduit vs. Content

The business value of the Internet of Things is predicated upon the ability to aggregate device data streams from smart, connected things for business insight, process optimization, and effective decision making.

This means new business models should not focus not on the "plumbing" of the Industrial Internet of Things, or its *conduits*, but rather on the *content* that flows through them. This context-rich content is what drives the Industrial Internet of Things and allows forward-looking companies, such as those mentioned in this book, to create new business models—disruptive business models, if you like the term—that create differentiation and competitive advantage.

We discussed examples of transformational initiatives and outcome-oriented business results in the previous chapter.

Unfortunately, however, most industrial sectors have yet to mature to the level they are able to reap the full value of Industrial IoT content. The majority of companies venturing into this nascent territory still focus on device and Internet connectivity, in part because they have no choice, as many products were not designed originally with connectivity in mind.

Product companies must go through a number of steps to create an Industrial Internet of Things infrastructure and connect and secure devices before they are able to harvest meaningful value.

As the figure on the next page illustrates, product companies must design product that can be connected securely to the Internet; they need to shore up the infrastructure to connect and manage these devices, and create the data aggregation, analytics, and decision-support applications.

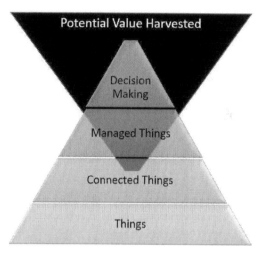

Business Value Realization

But while the early stages of this activity often represent the bulk of the investment in engineering and ICT, and gets more executive management attention, the outcome and value in creating an infrastructure of connected devices is limited to collecting, storing, and reporting on data. Indeed, while many product organizations will reap some benefits from this newly available, rich, real-time data from connected devices, the business value in just connecting and storing data is quite limited and doesn't scale to the full promise of the Internet of Things.

Only when the organization is able to mine the vast corpus of IoT information effectively, can it realize the long-term goal of making high-fidelity decisions, which we will discuss in the next chapter.

But before we move on, we should spend a little time discussing an important factor that is instrumental in enabling organizations to synthesize streams of device data and extract decision-making insight from them: the semantic frameworks that allow data to be shared and reused across application, enterprise, and community boundaries.

Semantic Standards Are Sorely Needed

When I use a word," Humpty Dumpty said, in a rather scornful tone, "it means just what I choose it to mean—neither more, nor less." "The question is," said Alice, "whether you can make words mean so many different things." "The question is," said Humpty Dumpty, "which is to be master—that's all.

Like the wine-making example we discussed in Chapter 3, and practically every Internet of Things implementation, the Industrial IoT is an aggregate of communicating and collaborating ecosystems. These ecosystems are comprised of heterogeneous and incompatible devices that carry different roles and exchange different types of information in various formats for a unique purpose defined and governed by the ecosystem in which the device belongs. Industrial IoT ecosystems, by their nature, are dynamic. They are heterogeneous, multi-modal networks that can be reconfigured, manually or automatically, for a task or a business purpose.

However, the multiple data streams of disparate devices cannot be simply combined into a single flow, nor can a collection of the dissimilar applications communicating with these devices be simply daisy-chained to exploit information that uses dissimilar data structures and incompatible data representations.

The Internet of Things, especially the Industrial Internet of Things, depends on data interoperability. That means not only compatible and interoperable data protocols are needed, but also, more critically, common data models and semantics so that information from dissimilar sources and functions can be linked, aggregated, and harmonized to form an Internet of Things solution.

Connectivity technology to facilitate the transmission of information to and from connected assets is relatively straightforward and inexpensive, and is getting more so by the day. In addition to the ubiquity of the TCP/IP Internet protocol, which is universally available, there are numerous wired and wireless standards[18] in place to connect industrial devices. And new device-interfacing and connectivity standards continue to emerge and evolve. That is the nature of innovation.

Data communication standards are that based on syntactic or simple binary data models facilitate easy data exchange but do not provide machine-interpretable meanings to the data. They do not address—not sufficiently, anyway—the intricacies of poor data interoperability.

Dr. Richard Soley, the Executive Director of the Industrial Internet Consortium, doesn't think the problem facing the industry is a lack of data communication standards:

> *There are already standards for how you move bits and bytes over the network. I don't believe in building standards until you know what you need them for. And I don't believe you know what you need them for until you've built a system. I am pretty sure that where we need standards is at the semantic level.*

Data semantic standards are critical to support the inevitable heterogeneity of Internet of Things devices and the data they collect. Moreover, the dynamic and auto-self-configured nature of Industrial IoT networks suggests that the meaning of the data and its application can also change across domain spaces and over time.

Operationally, semantic models serve to enhance resource discovery and management, and information interoperability, processing, analysis, and reasoning, i.e., decision making. Furthermore, the Industrial IoT foundation should accelerate the development of open-source implementations of standard protocol stacks using a variety of hardware and software such as the OpenWSN[19] project.

But let's not lose sight of the ultimate goal of interoperability, which is to provide the transparency to create rich multidisciplinary context that helps the organization make faster and better decisions.

Chapter Takeaways

- Every product and every person is becoming a connected node in an omnipresent connected cloud. Connectivity is being commoditized.

- The value of the Industrial Internet of Things is not in connectivity. It is in the organizational capacity to aggregate, mine, and put into action complex, multidisciplinary information originating from connected devices.

- The collective multidisciplinary information generated by smart, connected devices of the Internet of Things facilitates the "Wisdom of Things."

- The ability to utilize the Internet of Things effectively and efficiently is hinged upon data interoperability.

- Lack of data interoperability standards forces companies to invest in data translation and processing before they can realize business value from the Industrial Internet of Things. Semantic frameworks are sorely needed.

5

Making High-Fidelity Decisions

I knew who I was this morning, but I've changed a few times since then.
—ALICE

The value, or the utility, of information we use in making most business-related decisions isn't static; it is dynamic and changes over time.

In many situations, the general rule of decision making is to act promptly and decisively upon the arrival of new information. For instance, if a machine on the manufacturing line has drifted out of spec and starts spewing bad parts, it should be shut down immediately. Then, it needs to be repaired expeditiously in order to restore production as soon as possible. In this example, the impact, or the business value, of the decision is the highest when a quick and decisive action is taken. The longer we wait to shut down production, the more defective parts are going to be produced and scrapped.

As Lee Iacocca, the auto executive best known for steering the Chrysler Corporation away from bankruptcy toward record profits in the 1980s, once observed:

> *Even a correct decision is wrong when it was taken too late.*

But frequently, decision makers do not have enough information to make such quick decisions reliably. They need additional information to diagnose the problem and isolate its root cause. They need more comprehensive context to allow them to assess the situation in order to weigh alternate responses and make the right decision, as the following illustration shows.

Back at our manufacturing line, if there are multiple machines and processes that are responsible for part manufacturing, any one of which might be the culprit for those defective parts, then we need to consider several options before we can take action, because shutting down the entire line and restarting it will be too costly. We might need to spend time collecting and analyzing information to create sufficient context to make the right decision. In other words, the more time we spend on analyzing the problem (within reason, of course), the better decisions we are able to make. The *utility* of this kind of information *improves over time.*

We realize, therefore, that often there is a conflict between the need to make a quick decision that yields a greater business impact (but risk making an incorrect decision) and the need to make sure sufficient information and context were used to make the correct decision, as illustrated in the simple schematic below.

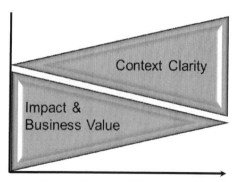

Time-Value of Information

Every decision maker, whether operating a production machine on the shop floor or working in the corporate corner office, needs to have information context to make the right decision—context that is complete, relevant, error-free, and sufficiently up-to-date. A trustworthy context that decision makers will use consistently.

The context to support high-fidelity decision making needs to incorporate operational and business data that you may not necessarily think about in the context of the Industrial Internet of Things: for instance, inventory levels, financials, market intelligence, and so forth. This data—together with IoT-generated data—is essential to making correct decisions such as the one described earlier. An example may be useful:

Attending to the problem on our manufacturing line, let's say that rectifying the problem requires a manufacturing process change or even a redesign. If the decision is made to affect the changes immediately, the factory may be left with expensive work-in-progress inventory and, perhaps, unable to meet contractual obligations with suppliers of raw materials. On the other hand, making and shipping these parts will most certainly result in additional warranty costs. Which is the better course of action?

An up-to-the-minute comprehensive decision-making context allows decision makers to consult business systems to understand inventory levels, supplier obligations, and other information to make a determination as far as the optimal point in time to implement the necessary design changes.

#YourProductSucks: Humans as Sensors

As we discussed earlier, the consistent ability to make and sustain high-fidelity business and operational decisions requires that decision makers, at all levels, have access to a rich, multidisciplinary context that represents the complete state of a supply chain, line operation, or asset performance. In many instances, this information is, indeed, generated by sensors and other connected devices at the edge of the IoT network. But we must also recognize that while this data is critically important, it may not always be sufficient to guarantee that the product organization is capable of making accurate and long-lasting decisions.

Today, owners and users of all types of products turn to the Internet's private and public forums and social media to look for information, seek advice from peers, and share their experiences and opinions with anyone who listens. Despite common misconception, this is not the exclusive domain of the young and always-connected generation. Forums to share information and seek advice about products have been around from the early days of the Internet and are used by casual users (quite often to complain about a product or a company) as well as professionals.

One of the earlier examples of such a professional forum is the International Automotive Technicians Network[20] that started back in 1995, at the early dawn of the Internet era. The iATN is a global network of independent automotive technicians that exchange information about car repairs—in particular, older models that are no longer covered by the manufacturer's warranty and are usually serviced by independent repair shops rather than by authorized dealers. during its 20-plus-year history, the iATN has grown to over 85,000 members in 167 countries, with cumulative professional experience of over 2 million years!

Initially, automakers didn't pay much attention to the iATN. But, over time, they realized that the conversations on the group's website had a wealth of information about vehicles' quality and durability, diagnostic and repair information, and—by inference— important hints about consumer satisfaction.

Even more exciting for automakers was the fact that they could glean similar technical and business information about competitors' products. Little by little, auto manufacturers started eavesdropping on these conversations, first anonymously, and eventually joining the discussions.

Today, the same is happening across numerous both formal, professional groups and open-to-all social media channels. Short-form chatting and microblogging capabilities provide consumers easy avenues to share opinions and experiences, and ask questions and get advice from peers as well as perfect strangers, all at the click of a mouse. Product companies from all industrial sectors like Caterpillar, General Motors, Toyota, and Whirlpool are monitoring and participating in social media forums and continually improving their social media analytics tools to learn what customers think of specific products, identify quality problems, and increase the accuracy of sales predictions.

Humans are becoming IoT sensors!

Shortening Latency of Information

In a 2015 letter to General Electric's shareholders[21] GE's CEO, Jeffrey Immelt, wrote:

We must be in the world of ideas, so we must remain contemporary and paranoid.

When multiple devices are connected and communicating information about their current state—whether automatically, by request from a centralized back-office system, or, perhaps, by a human when additional information is needed—the Internet of Things is facilitating two critical elements of decision making:

- Providing rich, multidisciplinary information from multiple sources.
- Ensuring this information is available in a timely fashion, whether real-time or delivered on-demand.

To paraphrase futurist and science fiction writer William Gibson[22], the information is here, it's just not evenly distributed. The Internet of Things *shortens the latency of information* and delivers better and richer context for higher-fidelity decisions. And once the Industrial Internet of Things infrastructure and business processes are in place, it continues to enhance and enrich the context at no incremental cost.

Accelerating the time to rich multidisciplinary contexts is one of the greatest promises of the Internet of Things: the ability to accelerate a company's innovation cycle, which we will discuss in the next chapter.

Chapter Takeaways

- The value, or the utility, of information we use in making most business-related decisions isn't static; it is dynamic and changes over time.

- The Internet of Things shortens the latency of information and delivers better and richer context for long-lasting, higher-fidelity decisions.

- The Industrial IoT isn't exclusively about data flowing from industrial equipment connected to the Internet. Effective decision making requires the synthesis of device- and non-device-generated data, including business systems and social media

- Once in place, the IoT continues to enhance and enrich the decision-making context throughout the product lifecycle at no incremental cost.

- Major industrial product companies monitor and analyze user inputs and social media to learn what customers think, identify quality problems, and increase the accuracy of sales forecasts.

The Outcome Economy

6

IoT and the
Innovation Cycle

*If you don't know where you are going
any road can take you there.*
—THE CHESHIRE CAT

In the emerging new world of the Industrial Internet of Things, we picture multiple devices and machines, ranging from manufacturing machinery to cars and household appliances, that are always connected and communicating with one another. We envision intelligent software-controlled products that operate semi-autonomously and deliver exciting new capabilities and engage customers via innovative business models.

Are the smart connected devices that make up the Industrial Internet of Things the same machines and apparatuses we know and understand today, only connected to the Internet? Or do we need a new way of thinking about the operations and features of the products of the future? Do we need a different engineering approach to design these products?

As I've emphasized throughout this book, mere device connectivity isn't the point. Connectivity is already an expected, innate capability of most products and systems. We need to think beyond connectivity; we need to focus on the business value of the Industrial Internet of Things, and understand the relationships between design disciplines and the business.

Design for the Business of the Internet of Things

For decades, product companies have invented different ways to erect barriers to market entry that restrict new entrants from competing in an industry or market. Many companies, startups in particular, bet on technology innovation, patents, and licenses as a deep protective moat around their products castles. Others develop cost advantage by leveraging economies of scale, low-cost suppliers, and manufacturing and supply chain efficiencies.

But these advantages are difficult to maintain over time. Companies depend on the same technology and cost advantage barriers they have been using for a long time, and become complacent, until a radical and disruptive new technology or approach to business moves the battlefield to a different front.

With technology barriers getting lower, and low-cost competition challenging the old cost advantage tactic, forward-looking product companies should avoid engaging in a never-ending pursuit of cost-cutting measures. Instead, they should guide business innovation in the direction of value-based outcomes. They should favor investments in technology innovations that offer a business outcome advantage rather than a technology advantage. As Michael Bayler, in his book *The Liquid Enterprise*,[23] suggests:

> *Until innovations are fully contextualized both within the business, and in their optimal location on The Network, they remain inventions whose value remains latent.*

This may seem a bit abstract. After all, don't all products reflect the business environment for which they are designed? Frequently this is not the case. All too often, the business user (or the end customer) is forced to restructure around the features and limitations of a newly-introduced product simply because not enough attention was given by the designers to the business environment.

The design of an Industrial Internet of Things device should first and foremost articulate the role of the device in a business solution and how it might influence operational strategy and decision making throughout its lifecycle.

Product designers and business owners need not only to define the basic functionality that forms classes of connected and collaborative physical devices, but, in many instances, the physical architecture of these devices needs to reflect the operational model and the role of the IoT device in the business value chain. In other words, the intended business model should influence and guide the design, not the other way around.

Again, it's quite possible that these ideas sound a bit abstract, so let me give you an example. Equipment maintenance, which often serves as the poster child of Industrial Internet of Things, is an excellent illustration.

Design for Service and Maintenance

In many—if not most—product organizations, the chief objective during the early phases of design is meeting the design goals set by the marketing team. The engineering team focuses on resolving and optimizing design goals, such as functionality and reliability, against constraints such as manufacturing costs and environmental compliance. But seldom do these goals and constraints look farther into the product lifecycle. Specifically, design engineers do not usually take into account the service and maintenance aspects of the new product.

What happens when equipment service and maintenance considerations are neglected early on? Let's view it from the perspective of the ability of the newly designed equipment to fulfill its intended business outcome.

The following anecdotes are from real-world commercial products that I've been personally involved in developing or reviewing. These examples illustrate the negative impact of such a myopic view on service operations:

- The fault diagnostics tools are unable to isolate the root cause of equipment failure down to a single field-replaceable unit (FRU). Consequently, the service technician is inclined to replace multiple parts, prolonging the repair process and inflating its cost.

- The service technician is unfamiliar with the location and configuration of the piece of equipment that requires service and, therefore, does not have the proper service information, spare parts, and tools to perform effective repair. The technician may have to make multiple trips between the site and the office to complete the job.

- In an attempt to reduce the physical footprint of the product, product designers buried certain FRUs deep inside the machine, again, resulting in excessive repair time.

- The stage-gate approach to product development (which we will discuss in the next chapter) "froze" the design before service planners had the opportunity to evaluate the design and improve its serviceability.

How can product companies change this? Here are some examples (based, again, on actual experience) that illustrate design thinking enabled by the Industrial Internet of Things from an equipment-maintenance point of view:

- Onboard and remote diagnostics, and remote software update tools are designed to meet aggressive service level agreements (SLAs) for equipment uptime and service responsiveness. This is an opportunity for the service organization to improve the profitability of extended service contracts.

- Remote and onboard diagnostics are aligned with hardware modularity, FRUs, and spare part inventory management policies. After all, there's little utility in identifying a failure remotely unless it can be mapped to an available spare part.

- The placement and access to parts that are prone to failure is optimized, and the use of special tools is minimized in order to simplify and accelerate repairs.

- Remote monitoring and diagnostic systems help maximize the utilization of technical support experts and allows more flexible allocation of the available field service personnel.

- Back-end systems are designed to take advantage of machine-generated data to assist in diagnostics and capture operations and failure data, which are then used to improve the design of current and future products.

Retrofitting Old Equipment

As I often point out to those who have an overly rosy view of the potential size of the Industrial Internet of Things market, the growth in that space is gated by the ability to connect and incorporate existing manufacturing assets into the Industrial IoT network.

The average age of industrial equipment in the U.S. is approximately 12 years, the highest since 1938.[24] Many of these factory floor manufacturing machines and industrial equipment lack the basic functionality that enables them to be connected to the Internet and be monitored remotely, yet, they still have a very long service life ahead of them. The business rationale of replacing these aging, yet functional and productive machines sooner than absolutely necessary may be difficult to justify.

All too often, the audience's suggestion is to retrofit the aging factory machinery, assembly lines, and manufacturing assets by adding sensors, data acquisition electronics, and communication capabilities so they can become smart, connected machines overnight. In most cases, this type of retrofitting is quite impossible or, at the very least, is highly impractical.

Simply super-gluing a sensor onto a piece of working equipment and connecting it to the Internet isn't a workable solution. The precise placement of a sensor may require mechanical redesign and will surely necessitate expensive onsite visits to perform the work, one piece of equipment at a time.

More importantly, retrofitting equipment while in service means taking it out of production for significant amounts of time, which, for most manufacturing companies, isn't a viable option at all.

Therefore, when assessing the business case for implementing an Industrial Internet of Things transformation, especially in a manufacturing and production machinery setup, organizations should evaluate the portfolio of installed assets under three general categories:

1. Business processes representing the best business outcome potential from an Industrial IoT transformation. Initiate an Industrial Internet of Things project.
2. Non-critical business processes and machinery that will see minimal return from becoming IoT-networked and are not worth upgrading. Let these aging assets reach the planned end-of-life and then reassess.

3. The remaining assets may warrant retrofitting only after careful technical and business analysis.

We will resume the conversation about the equipment modernization cadence of the industrial equipment industry and how it will influence the adoption of the Industrial Internet of Things in Chapter 10. But first, let's continue the discussion on product innovation and designing products for the Industrial Internet of Things, in the next chapter.

Chapter Takeaways

- The design of an Industrial Internet of Things device should define the role of the device as a component in a business solution and articulate how it will support the intended business outcomes.

- Design for the *business* of the Internet of Things should guide not only the functional requirements of products, but also the architectural modularity and business ecosystem.

- Equipment maintenance and field service operations are still some of the better articulated Industrial IoT applications. The complex relationships and interactions between serviceability, diagnostics, product modularity, and service operations can be used as a template for a "design for IoT" approach.

- Large segments of industrial equipment currently in operation is old and cannot be connected to the Internet, delaying the growth of the Industrial Internet of Things.

- Retrofitting aging equipment is not always cost-effective. Industrial companies should use a methodical approach to determine the types of production equipment that will provide a reasonable return if retrofitted to be connected an IoT subnetwork.

7

Design for IoT or Design by IoT?

Now, here, you see, it takes all the running you can do, to keep in the same place. If you want to get somewhere else, you must run at least twice as fast as that!"

—THE RED QUEEN

You are probably not aware of it but, in all likelihood, your product organization suffers from acute myopia—almost all product organizations do. What I mean by myopia is that once your product is sold or installed in the field, you lose sight of its performance, how users are interacting with it, and how well it meets your customers' expectations, as well as your business portfolio market targets.

In fact, probably unbeknownst to your company's management, that organizational myopia set in much earlier, during the collection and formulation of market and functional requirements for your product.

In many product companies, market analysis and functional requirements tend to be based on incomplete, biased, and out-of-date views of the market, consumers, and competitors, and are highly predisposed to subjective human interpretation.

A simple example might surprise you. Practically all new cars come equipped with CD players. Some, usually higher-end models, offer additional MP3- or iPhone-compatible plugs. But do carmakers know how often the CD players in these cars are used? Do customers use the physical iPhone connection? Or, perhaps, CDs and physically connected devices are outdated and are being supplanted by wireless Bluetooth-connected devices?

Detailing requirements for a complex technology product is not a small feat. If you are a manufacturer of complex products with a long development cycle, such as automobiles or heavy equipment, the magnitude and complexity of detailed product requirements can be quite perplexing. For example, a typical major automotive supplier receives about 300 different electronic documents from its suppliers, each holding some 20 or 30 pages of detailed functional, physical and regulatory information for a new system. Thousands of individual and intricately interdependent requirements are stated using different engineering disciplines and organization styles, and are managed by an assortment of requirements management tools. No matter how detailed these requirement documents may be, they can only represent a limited number of user groups, market segments, and operating conditions.

Where the Innovation Funnel Fails

Part of the problem is the use of the "innovation funnel" paradigm,[25] a widely used method of sifting innovation wheat from chaff. The innovation funnel methodology guides an idea from concept to reality by converging multiple requirements and design ideas into a well-defined cohesive product that meets market needs in an economical, manufacturable, serviceable, and environmentally sustainable form.

The concept of the innovation funnel is quite straightforward and easy to comprehend. But it's also conceptually flawed and could result in developing the wrong product with the wrong features.

Why?

The innovation funnel is fundamentally a linear, forward-feeding process. It starts with an ideation phase, often described simplistically as "filling the pipeline with ideas." Then, these ideas go through multiple iterative assessment and refinement phases to discarding some of these ideas and selecting others that will eventually get approved, developed, and launched. Each phase and each step in the process is bound by "gates":[26] once the development passes through a phase gate, the process marches forward; there's no turning back.

The entire focus of the innovation funnel and the stage-gate process is to pare down a large number of different ideas to a smaller and manageable number by discarding less critical and less feasible product ideas. But how do you know which requirements are weaker? How do you pick the winners? How do you know for certain that the car's CD player is, indeed, desired by customers and has not become relic like the 8-track and cassette players?

To be fair and precise, the innovation funnel does encourage market studies, benchmarks, and focus groups, which can be highly valuable in vetting product concepts and requirements. But, all too often, these studies and research activities are highly biased towards the original assumptions established by the product leadership beforehand. Furthermore, they are frequently predisposed to subjective human interpretation, a "not invented here" attitude, and internal bickering, as in the case of General Motors' Pontiac Aztek presented in the following page.

Finally, armed with detailed requirements (or, as detailed as the team managed), the project progresses through the timeline and marches deeper into the funnel. Design concepts are simulated and vetted, and prototypes are built and tested. But, here again, these activities are conducted in the relative darkness of static—and often stale—voluminous sets of product requirements.

But the innovation process marches on, gaining momentum, and the organization becomes more myopic. It becomes less able and willing to receive and consider new information from outside. In fact, innovation funnel advocates and project management experts like to talk about "freezing" requirements and design decisions and push the process firmly towards the next gate.

And while the project continues and management focuses on internal goals and measurements, much is happening outside the funnel's impenetrable walls.

By the time the new product finally reaches the market, the original requirements may very well be a couple of years old. Much has changed during that time: a new competitor appeared in the market, customer preferences have shifted, and new technology threatens to make your product offering less appealing. Only you didn't see it—or, worse, the design was too far down the line so you were unable to respond to the changes effectively.

The Sad Story of the Pontiac Aztek

Here is another, lesser-known but highly illustrative example: the maligned General Motors Pontiac Aztek, which was first shown to the public in 1999. Despite plenty of evidence that the market would have no interest in the new car, Don Hackworth, the executive in charge of product development, refused to concede. Bob Lutz, GM's iconic executive, quoted Mr. Hackworth: "Look. We've all made up our minds that the Aztek is gonna be a winner. It's gonna astound the world."[27]

The Pontiac Aztek, as we now know, was a miserable failure.

But that wasn't the end of the Aztek's story.

While new car sales during its 5-year production run were an abysmal 120,000 units, fifteen years later, the Pontiac Aztek became a favorite among young used-car buyers. In 2015, the car accounted for 25 percent of used cars bought by millennials.[28] (Some credit this to Walter White, a character from the popular TV series *Breaking Bad*,[29] who drove a custom-painted greenish Aztek for most of the series.)

The irony is that GM missed the market once, with the original Aztek by ignoring market inputs, and then it missed it again by not recognizing the signals revealing opportunity among millennials.

Automakers are spending billions of dollars[30] to design and market new cars. Despite such massive investments in market research and advertising, automakers prove repeatedly that they hardly understand their buyers. Not only do some cars sell very poorly and never reach profitability, but many successful models sold best in a vastly different consumer segment than the one for which they were targeted.

The lesson from the history of the Aztek highlights not only the need to make decisions based on objective and timely information, but also the fact that even this type of evidence may not necessarily be enough to overpower human biases, "not invented here" attitudes, and internal politics and turf battles. As Don Hackworth declared, "I don't want any negative comments about this vehicle. None. Anybody who has bad opinions about it, I want them off the team."[31]

IoT-Enabled Innovation

So, how do you counterbalance the sort of bias that can blindside an organization's ability to innovate effectively? And, most importantly, how do you do this at a time when the pace of new product introductions and technology adoption is accelerating, demanding that product organizations act faster and faster in response to market pressures and reduce the high risk of innovation?

Simply put, product organization must change our approach to innovation. They need to:

- Scale fast, fail fast, recalibrate fast.
- Build exactly what customers want.
- Present and vet new ideas with a working product and live customers.

Discussing the opportunity in the Internet of Things, James Heppelmann, CEO of IoT Company PTC, observes:

> *The Internet of Things is a new opportunity. The reason why companies connect products to the Internet is to improve service, operations and design, by having feedback loops from products deployed in the field. Think of this as evidence-based PLM [product lifecycle management] that is used to improve design, operation and service of products during their lifecycle downstream of manufacturing.*

Your product organization does not have a true and complete view of your product and how customers are using it, unless you continue to observe it through its lifecycle.

The Industrial Internet of Things and the digitization of the value chain radically redefines how well we understand current products and customers, and how we use this insight to accelerate innovation and develop new products and services. Always-connected products provide a real-time view that enables broad and deep insight across multiple markets, product configurations, and customer groups.

The Internet of Things offers a new approach to collect requirements and to understand what products and services are really being used and how, as Dr. Gahl Berkooz, Head of Data and Governance at Ford Motor Company, explains:

> *Requirements and architecture today are abstractions created by subject matter experts. Abstractions used to drive the design process should be replaced with actual data.*

Connected products in the Internet of Things allow an ongoing process of validating and refining the innovation process, from early market and functional requirements to lifetime continuous improvement, as the table on the next page shows. Think of this as a *perpetual focus group* for each and every key product lifecycle function.

The Internet of Things can have a significant impact on the way an organization innovates by providing rich, comprehensive, and nearly irrefutable empirical data about how a product is actually being used.

IoT-centric innovation enables agile, iterative, self-corrected innovation. It guides the development of product concepts and reduces the risk in product development and new product introduction.

Ford Motor Company is centering its future product innovation strategy around the synthesis and analysis of comprehensive multifaceted information: car-generated data, market intelligence garnered from social media, enterprise software tools, and traditional methods.

Dr. Berkooz explains how he foresees this strategy as a fundamental shift in how the company uses information to improve innovation and drive better product related decisions:

Ford's data supply chain will provide a quantum reduction in time to insight and will fundamentally change how products are engineered.

	Traditional Strategy	IoT Strategy
Concept	· Market experts · Focus groups · Benchmarks	· Consumer behavioral analytics · Rapid concept testing via social media
Requirements	· Requirements documents · Specifications	· Actual product use and performance
Design	· Product context	· Ecosystem
Verification & Validation	· Predefined use cases · Test specifications	· Customer behavior using similar and competitive products · Sensor data · Actual use data

IoT-Guided Innovation

Let's finish this chapter by stopping by a Coca-Cola Freestyle vending machine.[32] This machine offers over 100 drink options in a single machine. A "Create Your Own Mix" smartphone Freestyle app lets fans create and save custom combinations, and then scan the app at a participating machine, which will, in turn, pour their very own mix which they can share with friends.

The Freestyle vending machine tracks and reports what flavors are most sought after and when it is about to run out of syrup.

And, of course, loyal consumers can earn badges and win prizes.

This is quite an improvement from the jerry-rigged Coke vending machine at Carnegie Mellon University I mentioned in Chapter 2.

The Freestyle vending machine is a great example of a product designed with the mindset of the business of IoT we discussed in the previous chapter. In this case, the product—the business outcome—extends beyond an efficient apparatus to dispense Coke products. It accomplishes much more:

- It promotes brand affinity.
- It offers better understanding of consumer preferences by location, gender, and age (subject to user permission, of course).

- It is a platform to experiment with new flavors at minimum market research investment and lower risk.

In short, it's the perfect focus group: always on and engaged, always aware of its behaviors, and always informing you of how to customize and personalize the product for the market—which now provides the perfect platform for us to take the next step and discuss how to extract business value from this data.

Chapter Takeaways

- Traditional product innovation and development methods such as the innovation funnel are slow, rigid, and not responsive enough to rapidly changing market needs. As a result, many products fail to meet market expectations.

- Connected products give organizations a true and complete view of both products and customers throughout their lifecycles, forming a perpetual focus group to improve current and future products.

- The Internet of Things enables agile self-calibrating innovation: scale fast, fail fast, recalibrate fast.

- Product organizations should have a strategy to synthesize multidisciplinary information from multiple sources: IoT devices, market intelligence garnered from social media, enterprise software tools, etc.

- Even good data does not protect against human biases (but it can certainly help).

8

Predictive Analytics: Extracting Value Out of Data

It's a poor sort of memory that only works backwards.
                    —THE WHITE QUEEN

I
f there is one recurring theme and promise in the narrative of the Industrial Internet of Things, it is the grandiose vision of predictive analytics, most frequently that of predictive maintenance. The vision is quite simple and very compelling. But our ability to

reach the pot of gold at the end of the rainbow may still be in the future.

The outcome economy is hinged upon the ability of machines and instruments to produce a desired business outcome: generate power, drill quarter-inch holes, transmit vineyard microclimate information, and so forth. Therefore, keeping these machines and instruments up and running is of the utmost importance. And many Internet of Things systems and solutions are designed and cost-justified in the context of their ability to improve equipment uptime in the most cost-effective manner.

But before we begin, it's worthwhile—in fact, it's imperative—that we spend a little time to understand the different approaches and practiced of equipment maintenance and how they can leverage Internet connectivity.

One Goal, Many Flavors

Condition-Based Maintenance

A common method to reduce unscheduled service interruptions employed by the majority of maintenance organizations is one form or another of reliability-centered maintenance (RCM).[33] RCM is a systematic preventative approach to conduct routine maintenance tasks designed to confirm and preserve important functionality before a hard failure occurs. Although you may not have heard of RCM, you are likely practicing it: the periodic replacement of the oil in your car is based on a reliability-driven schedule.

While generally effective, RCM is hardly efficient; maintenance activities take place on schedule, whether they are needed or not. As a statistics-based strategy, RCM is not completely failsafe and tends to be wasteful, especially in mission-critical applications, where frequent maintenance activities are performed to maintain high level of readiness.

But what if we had a way to perform preventative service only when it was truly needed, just before the component fails?

Industrial IoT equipment can be instrumented to gather information about its state: temperature, pressures, speed, vibration, and any data that provides objective evidence about the machine's well-being. This information can then be used by the service organization to determine the severity of the situation, when a trip (or a "truck roll" in service parlance) is justified, and what maintenance activities are warranted.

For instance, Tivall,[34] a maker of frozen food products from vegetable sources, uses a predictive maintenance software from Augury,[35] a vendor that boasts the clever tag line, "machines talk, we listen." The company reported savings of $120,000 when the software detected two critical mechanical malfunctions that were repaired during a planned maintenance cycle and prevented a major failure and line shutdown.

Predictive Maintenance

Instrumented and connected industrial equipment forms the foundation of the holy grail of the Industrial IoT: predictive maintenance. Predictive maintenance systems are comprised of complex algorithms that combine historical and real-time data to identify and help circumvent critical failure events before they occur. Predictive modeling can identify what equipment is going to fail and how soon, advise about the likely cause of the failure, and prioritize the handling of the impending failure.

General Electric's SmartSignal[36] predictive software is a good example. Demonstration of the system in a fossil fuel power plant underscored the potential benefits of condition monitoring and predictive maintenance. In one instance, the software used a year's worth of data to analyze the behavior of a coal unit's condensate pump. While there were no externally visible signs of failure of the pump, the analysis detected anomalies in the data that indicate a pump failure in progress. The total economic loss of this type of pump failure was estimated at over $2 million, while the cost of preemptive repairs was around $150,000.

A Nuts and Bolts Discussion

These examples of successful Industrial Internet of Things projects are impressive and the economic value they deliver is outstanding indeed. But the path to implementing robust and scalable industrial-grade predictive models is fraught with numerous real-world challenges. Predictive diagnostics models, machine learning, and other techniques that attempt to extract knowledge from complex machine data and provide proactive advice are extremely difficult to build and maintain.

The most prominent challenge stems from the broad variability in the installed equipment, even among seemingly identical pieces of equipment. A couple of examples will illustrate this point.

Consider a fleet of identical trucks rolling off the assembly line and being delivered to different customers. Some of these trucks are used for long-distance cargo hauling, covering great distances, and cruising long hours at highway speeds. Other trucks make short trips in start-and-stop city traffic. Over time, the different traffic conditions, cargo loads, and even the driver's driving patterns cause these trucks to age and wear differently. Add to those factors the inconsistent service and maintenance practices that often do not follow the manufacturer's recommendations, and these trucks are no longer close facsimiles of each other, or the original truck that was used as the model for the predictive data analysis.

Of course, the same type of challenge exists in stationary equipment. The operational "signature" of a diesel engine used to power an emergency generator infrequently and at a constant speed will look very different from that of an identical engine that operates long hours under variable loads. The as-maintained configuration and field-installed options of like products are as critical to accurate analysis and diagnostic recommendations as the raw telemetry data.

Because the behavior of individual units—both during normal operation and when a subsystem fails—is not static and changes due to normal wear and tear, modifications, operator interaction, maintenance practices, and numerous other factors, the predictive analytics models must be updated continually—manually or programmatically—to respond to these changes. Many attempts to build scalable maintenance applications have failed because they grossly underestimated the effort and organizational changes that are required to keep these systems up to date, leading to their eventual demise.

Building reliable failure prediction models for highly engineered assets has proven difficult. These models require large data sets that are continually updated to reflect the ongoing changes caused by built-in variability, wear and tear, and configuration changes over the life of these machines.

Extracting Value From Data

Siemens Digitalization Office and Siemens Digital Services[37] can offer a perspective of a pervasively connected industrial world and how analytic and predictive software tools are extracting actionable business information from device data.

Siemens's Sinalytics Internet of Things platform connects some 300,000 devices throughout the company's various operating units and production facilities. The system aggregates and analyzes data locally or at a centralized data warehouse, mashing it up with business data and business process orchestration rules.

You may recall the contract for guaranteed on-time train schedules between Renfe Rail and Siemens we described in the beginning of the book. Some 160 Siemens maintenance experts use this type of data analysis to maximize the availability of Renfe's trains and deliver the contracted outcome to passengers.

Siemens' approach to advanced predictive analytics highlights the importance of synthesizing multiple data sources, human expertise, and business best practices. For this reason, Siemens chose to establish a corporate-level Digitalization Office rather than view the Industrial Internet of Things as yet another ancillary product functionality.

In our conversation, Alexander Epple, R&D Strategy Manager at Siemens Digitalization Office, emphasized the multidisciplinary principles of the company's comprehensive digitalization[38] strategy:

> *Success of a predictive maintenance system requires that we consider the data and physical models, as well as heuristics, business rules and understanding of market developments. When it comes to the specific applications and services, we recruit domain experts from the different business units and expert support from Corporate Technology. So it is not one big*

> *interdisciplinary team, but a mix of centralized platform development and decentralized application development.*

The Rise of Citizen Data Scientists

While digitalization may be a crucial part of organizations developing specialized in-house competencies, its greater promise is on making the flood of data available to every employee in meaningful ways.

However, the long and somewhat painful history of developing knowledge-intensive decision-support technologies, from the early days of artificial intelligence-driven expert systems to the heydays of knowledge management,[39] and today's advanced machine learning software, teaches us valuable lessons:

- Product information is highly dynamic. Wear and tear, changes in operation procedures, updated regulations, and other issues must be reflected in knowledge-based decision support systems. Systems that were successful in insulated lab conditions often fail because they are unable to keep up with rate and diversity of change.
- Systems that focus on algorithmic wizardry and do not give enough consideration to human and business processes (even when these systems are

able to outperform humans) tend to fail in the long run. User adoption of these systems tends to be poor, eroding the utilization of these systems and accelerating their demise.

These lessons are well-anchored in the observations of Edward Feigenbaum,[40] one of the early pioneers of artificial intelligence:

> *Intelligent systems derive their power from the knowledge they possess rather than from the specific formalisms and inference schemes they use.*

Feigenbaum's statement underscores the critical role of process and domain knowledge—whether built into the data analysis software or supplemented by human interpretation and inferencing capabilities. The very same sentiment was also echoed in Mr. Epple's observation about the ideal and practical composition of Industrial IoT project teams.

We realize, then, that making sense out of complex data and applying it in a complex operational and business context is not a trivial task and perhaps should not be relegated completely and blindly to automation. It may be argued that Internet of Things systems that can be integrated fully and effectively into the business process and help drive positive business outcomes need to involve human data scientists.

These data scientists work at the intersection of complex multidisciplinary data, advanced statistical modeling, technology domains, and business processes. They are conversant across different business units and business disciplines. But they are also in very short supply.

Luckily, data discovery and analysis tools that have traditionally been used manually by statisticians have advanced to a point where domain experts that know the business well but lack deep knowledge in data analysis can leverage them to perform analytical tasks that would previously have required the expertise of a highly skilled data scientist.

Unlike traditional data scientists, modern-day data scientists do not live in the ivory towers of academia, nor are they absent-minded PhDs hiding out of sight in some dark corporate basement. They are professionals who use off-the-shelf advanced analytics tools to make product- and business-related decisions. Market research company Gartner calls this new breed of knowledge workers "citizen data scientists."[41]

Citizen data scientists come from the line of business, product development, corporate business intelligence, and ICT. When in a group of multidisciplinary and domain experts, as practiced by Siemens Data Services, this approach enables faster time to analytics maturity.

It's worth reiterating the importance of citizen data scientist beyond their contribution to faster and possibly more accurate data analytics. The mere fact that the analysis and subsequent business operations decisions are created and endorsed by domain experts goes a long way towards reaching a broader audience, encouraging use, fostering collaboration, and accelerating time to value of the IoT solution.

But a word of caution is also due. As enterprise data is being "democratized"—as many IoT advocates like to describe the gush of new data—and the use of data analytics and visualization tools become not only much easier, but also expected by executive management, the lines between extracting useful information and generating pretty but utterly useless charts and graphs will undoubtedly blur. We need to be reminded of the cross-disciplinary team approach taken by companies like Siemens Digital Services, which forces discovery and analytics that center on domain-specific business value.

Learning Machines to the Rescue

By now, having read through the numerous examples of Industrial Internet of Things applications, the argument that rich, complex, and multidisciplinary data is the core of the Internet of Things should be abundantly clear.

We already discussed how Ford, General Electric, Rolls-Royce, and Siemens use advanced data analytics to extract valuable information from IoT-delivered data.

Indeed, industry giants and scores of smaller companies are pouring billions of dollars into the research and development of data analytics, artificial intelligence, and machine-learning algorithms.[42] IBM, Google, Microsoft (which, by the way, developed the Cortana data analytics algorithms used by Rolls-Royce's TotalCare system I described in Chapter 1), and many others are working to develop sophisticated tools to help manufacturers unlock the business value in the vast data repositories generated by the Industrial Internet of Things.

Despite rapid and impressive progress in machine learning systems, we are still in the early stages of this journey. We discussed earlier, in Chapter 4, the difficulties in overcoming data semantics incompatibilities; another challenge for data analytics software is dealing with fast-moving, unstructured, heterogeneous, input data.

While much of the work in this field does not necessarily translate into industry-ready decision-support applications—at least not yet—we are likely to see heightened activity and accelerated success in one-off industrial applications first, and eventually as generalized and reusable tools. Extensive work in artificial neural networks[43] and applying "brute force" computing[44] approaches to tasks that, until recently, were considered unsolvable using commercial means, not only is showing success, but also leading to large investments in startup companies and an increase in mergers and acquisitions activities.

In the same way that Google has allowed us to be our own professional researchers and librarians of the world's content, the fast evolution in data discovery and analytics tools is beginning to alter the landscape of business by bringing the power of the Internet of Things to every part of the business.

Chapter Takeaways

- Advanced hardware maintenance methods, such as condition-based maintenance and predictive maintenance, leverage Internet connectivity to improve equipment uptime and field service operations.

- Building efficient and effective predictive analytic systems is difficult. The dominant reasons slowing down progress are the extensive variability in equipment configurations and operating patterns, lack of semantic interoperability, and large volumes of fast-moving unstructured input data.

- Building effective analytic models require multidisciplinary teams from engineering, business, and data sciences.

- Data analytics tools and training must advance so that companies can leverage "citizen data scientists" more effectively.

- The majority of automated machine learning-based predictive software has yet to mature beyond one-off implementations. However, we should expect accelerated investments in these activities to yield more general-purpose and reusable tools.

The Outcome Economy

9

The Internet of Things and Digital Transformation

... it's no use going back to yesterday, because I was a different person then.

—ALICE

The Industrial Internet of Things appears to be in full swing, and technology innovations are certainly on its side. Hardware miniaturization, reduced power consumption, falling hardware prices, and ubiquitous wireless connectivity proliferate and power many new products and highly automated devices.

Then, new business models and novel ways to engage customers and interact with businesses promise to bring new customers and additional revenue streams. The confluence of these technologies and business models fuel the growth of the Industrial Internet of Things.

PTC's CEO Mr. Heppelmann highlights the role of technology innovations in driving this momentum:

> *Innovations across the technology landscape have converged to make smart, connected products technically and economically feasible. We can build solutions that previously were not cost-effective or even possible.*

As we see throughout this book, there are plenty of compelling arguments—both business-oriented and technology-induced—that the Industrial Internet of Things will, indeed, lead to a radical transformation in practically every business sector.

But without the appropriate context, i.e., the business rationale delineating the desired outcome, business transformation can be dangerously distracting and is bound to disappoint and fail. So, let's delve deeper into the business transformation sparked by the Industrial Internet of Things.

The Return of the Real-Time Enterprise?

Remember the real-time enterprise,[45] the concept in business systems design aspiring to improve organizational responsiveness that was popular in the first decade of the 21st century? Perhaps you remember them as sense-and-respond networks or on-demand enterprises.

Though not particularly well-defined, the primary objectives of the real-time enterprise can be summarized as follows:

- Reduce response times to market demands, including from customers and partners.
- Increase transparency across the enterprise instead of keeping information within separate organizational silos.
- Improve operational efficiencies and reduce costs thanks to process automation and enhanced process visibility across internal and external functions, including supply chain partners.

Sounds a lot like the aspirations of the Industrial Internet of Things, doesn't it?

Understanding the IoT Transformation

The Industrial Internet of Things delivers incrementally transformative value in several ways. It's helpful to view IoT-centric transformations along the following four stages, or dimensions, remembering these are, by and large, sequential and provide increasingly greater value:

- *Automate.* Embedded control software and device connectivity to automate operational and decision-making tasks.
- *Accelerate.* IoT as a means to shorten the latency of information. Remote access, augmented by data analytics and decision support systems, improves the organization's response time. The vast majority of Internet of Things implementations today are tactically focused on accelerating response times and only to some degree, on optimizing resource allocation.
- *Enhance.* Big data analytics, simulation software, and similar enterprise decision-support tools to optimize all aspects of the product lifecycle by mining enterprise data. Unlike the preceding two stages of IoT transformation, which are predominantly *retrospective* and tactically *reactive*, the depth and

breadth of information is leveraged to improve the fidelity of long-term *predictive* product design and operational decisions.

- **Engage.** The pinnacle of IoT-centric product strategy: connected products coupled with advanced decision-making processes transform traditional business models and engage customers via new fine-tuned, user-centric, outcome-based service offerings.

Restructuring the Value Chain

In his bestseller book, *Competitive Advantage: Creating and Sustaining Superior Performance*,[46] Harvard Business School professor Michael Porter describes the concept of the product value chain.

Porter's product value chain is a "general framework for thinking strategically about the activities involved in any business and assessing their relative cost and role in differentiation ... The value chain provides a rigorous way to understand the sources of buyer value that command a premium price, and why one product substitutes for another."

Porter views the manufacturing or service organization as a system, made up of sequentially organized subsystems, each with inputs, transformation processes, and outputs. These subsystems are responsible for the organization's primary value-generating activities: inbound logistics, operations, outbound logistics, marketing and sales, and service. In addition, secondary activities such as human resources, training, and ICT infrastructure are in place to support the primary value chain activities.

How does the Industrial Internet of Things support a company's value chain activities?

Value chain-based processes focus on understanding and creating customer value-add activities, and the process interfaces between these activities. But, these subsystems can inadvertently lead to the formation of technology, process, and functional and silos surrounded by insurmountable walls of business culture. I mentioned numerous examples of those organization silos throughout the book, and, in particular, in Chapter 7.

The IoT gives companies greater visibility to the myriad of value chain activities that transform inputs to outputs and move the product lifecycle forward. As we discussed in the previous chapter, it gives the organization greater ability to coalesce and analyze data from historical and transpiring value chain events—both negative and positive—and the agility to respond quickly and efficiently based on timely and objective data from across the value chain.

Again, a simple example will illustrate this point. Practically all product companies generate and store product service transactions across the value chain: customer service visits, warranty claims, sales orders, and so forth. But, all too often, these remain within the value chain function (and transaction management software systems) that have created them: service, warranty administration, and sales, respectively. However, a forward-looking product company will combine sales forecast, product service history, and real-time device data to project service operations load, forecast warranty repair costs, and optimize service parts inventory.

The information created by connected products and coupled with enterprise systems is ready to alter and reshape every activity in the organization's value chain. It both enables and requires more flexible and permeable boundaries and changes the traditional order in which value chain decisions are being made.

Consequently, as much as the Industrial Internet of Things helps improve the efficiency and agility of an organization's value chain operation, it is as fundamental in disrupting and rearranging Porter's original rigid incremental value chain model. Porter touches upon this idea, although not changing the principal value chain model, in *How Smart, Connected Products Are Transforming Companies*.[47]

At present, enterprises may not be amenable to redefining the traditional value chain boundaries. But as the practice of IOT continues to spread and business value is becoming evident, functional boundaries will shift to accommodate new functions and business practices.

Seizing Your Opportunity

Throughout this book, we discussed the numerous opportunities the Industrial Internet of Things offers, from better operational visibility via data analytics, to business disruption, different customer engagement models, and new revenue streams.

How do you find your opportunity in the vast landscape of the Industrial Internet of Things?

A convenient way—a necessary way, in fact—to chart a path forward is to focus on customer business outcomes.

Remember the digital vineyards we discussed in Chapter 3? Say you are a manufacturer of irrigation equipment. How do you take advantage of what the IoT has to offer? You have several options, building incrementally upon each other (refer to the illustration on the next page):

- *Sell irrigation equipment.* You are in the traditional *product* business.
- *Sell irrigation services.* In addition to selling irrigation system components, you install the irrigation system and the owner of the vineyard pays you a monthly fee for a service that guarantees regularly scheduled watering. You are now in the *product-as-service* category, which gives you long-term recurring revenue opportunities.
- *Smart, connected irrigation.* You utilize sensors and remote connectivity to optimize irrigation management and control the frequency and duration of irrigation based on current conditions and weather forecast. Your customers save water, reduce operating costs, and improve the health of the vineyards.
- *Connected ecosystem.* An extensive network of connected sensors maintains a detailed view of microclimate conditions such as ambient and soil

temperature and humidity, wind, rainfall, and leaf wetness. Back-end systems combine information from the vineyard, public information (for example, weather forecasts), and third-party partners (for example, a university database of pests and diseases). A collaborative ecosystem of service providers coordinates activities and adds value across the various stages of vineyard work.

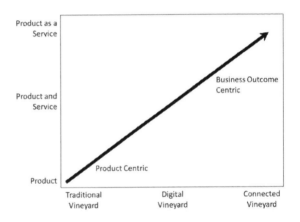

Smart, Connected Vineyards

Not Without Risks

Thus far in the book, I chose to concentrate on the benefits of the Industrial Internet of Things to companies' customers and their customers' customers. In particular, in this chapter, we spent much time on business model transformations that improve customer outcomes, and, consequently, give your organization a competitive advantage.

But some of these innovative business models don't come for free, and there are certain downsides and risks to consider.

It's obvious that a significant investment is needed in instrumentation and back-end systems before we are able to switch to an as-a-service model and take advantage of a renewable service contract. (Refer to Appendix II: *Return on Investment* at the end of the book for a short discussion about the return on IoT infrastructure investments.)

The advantage of an as-a-service model to customers is clear. But the more renewable services utilizing our own products and infrastructure we sell, the fewer products, repair services, and upgrades customer purchase.

Potentially, even a greater risk is spoiling the customer. Since adding features and services is easier and less expensive (this is the advantage of software-based functionality), customers might expect continued product improvements and additional features at a significantly lower cost—and even for free.

Even worse, as we progress towards the outcome economy, customers have less and less skin in the game. They do not invest in capital equipment, have not sunk money into custom development and systems integration, and, ultimately, their switching cost is very low. This is the primary reason why product organizations cannot rely on solving narrowly-defined tasks, no matter how difficult or lucrative they may be. They must build open and scalable systems that allow them to harness the power of partner ecosystems.

The Power of Ecosystems

Marshall Van Alstyne of Boston University once noted:[48]

> *Most companies compete by adding new features to products. They haven't been in the business of thinking of how to add new communities or network effects.*

Van Alstyne's observation highlights the core strength of the Industrial Internet of Things: the power of networked ecosystems.

The key to success in the era of Industrial Internet of Things is to shift the strategy away from tightly controlling products and supply chains, setting tall barriers to entry, and waging price wars aimlessly and in vain. The focus of product thinking must shift from inside the company to customers and partner ecosystems on the outside.

In the future, successful companies will create open and scalable systems that allow them to harness the power of partner ecosystems. They will orchestrate these ecosystems and set market exchanges based on open, standards-based, connected platforms and IoT devices.

A diverse partnership ecosystem will help organizations bridge gaps in product development and delivery, shorten time to value, and reduce risk. They will augment and enrich the portfolio of products and services, and bolster customer loyalty faster—and, in all likelihood, better, faster, and cheaper—than if these services were to be developed internally or acquired.

Connected partner ecosystems and open market exchanges create an agile environment to identify opportunities to gain and service customers and respond to market changes and competitive threats.

However, as you might expect, value chain disruptions, new customer engagement models, leveraging partnership ecosystems, and, of course, new technologies and product design methods, will have a profound impact on product companies, which we will discuss in the next section.

The Organization in Turmoil

Today's Industrial IoT narrative is highly technical and prefers to discuss issues surrounding the design of "smart" devices and connecting them to the Internet. But, as Peter Drucker notes in an essay in *Technology, Management and Society in the Twentieth Century*,[49] companies should pay as much attention to human, societal, and organizational issues:

> *We are becoming aware that the major questions regarding technology are not technical but human questions.*

While the promise of the Industrial Internet of Things can be uplifting, and the economic upside is no doubt significant, the cost and impact of the changes in the organization— some necessary, others inevitable—cannot be overstated and certainly should not be ignored.

Fundamentally, traditional methods for making products and getting them to customers, many of which have not changed much for nearly a century, will have to change. And so will organizational structures.

Product companies will have to rethink their core competencies, organizational structures, and outsourcing strategies.

The observation that the Internet of Things will have a significant impact on future job requirements and skills in demand is intuitively obvious. Manufacturers will need to hire more software engineers. They will need professionals specialized in a range of new disciplines such as security, big data analytics, and decision support systems. And, in all likelihood, many new hires may not fit comfortably into a corporate culture dominated by traditional mechanical and electrical engineers.

There should be no doubt that the effect of the restructuring of the product design organization triggered by IoT technology will be felt not only by the product design and engineering organization. Thinking back about Porter's value chain concept, it becomes obvious that the Industrial Internet of Things must touch nearly all value chain functions in the organization.

Rather than reiterating the role of the IoT in the more obvious value chain activities, let's discuss one organizational function that is likely less aware of how it will be forced to innovate and transform: the sales and marketing organization.

Sales and marketing staff will need learn how to position their product and service offerings not as individual pricelist items but rather as components of a connected business system, some of which may be provisioned, orchestrated, and operated by partners or even competitors. For instance, referring back to the connected vineyard examples discussed in Chapter 3, a connected vineyard requires business orchestration and collaboration between the sensor network installer, providers of external information databases, and fertilization and irrigation service providers. For instance, Rolls-Royce's TotalCare partners include Delta and Lufthansa—both offer maintenance, repair, and overhaul (MRO) services that compete with each other and with those of Rolls-Royce.

Another change will be learning to sell together with those partners, focusing on collaborative solutions whose value is defined primarily by future outcomes and adherence to service level commitments. Undoubtedly, this new and very unfamiliar scheme will necessitate that sales goals and incentives will be tweaked to accommodate complex revenue-sharing models.

Chapter Takeaways

- Convergence of technologies and new business models make smart, connected products technically and economically more feasible than ever. Product and customer connectivity give companies unprecedented insight into all value chain activities.

- The strength of the IoT stems from its networked ecosystems. Diverse ecosystems help organizations create and participate in a broader portfolio of customer-value services. They help bridge gaps in product and services portfolios, shorten time to value, and reduce risks.

- New business and customer engagement models require that traditional value chain boundaries, including with external functions such as supply chain, become more flexible and permeable.

- While as-a-service model offers great customer value and recurring revenue stream for product companies, it also lowers the barrier to customer abandonment.

- IoT-induced enterprise transformations are radical and involve multiple value chain functions. While some are obvious, the impact on others is less noticeable, yet, it is as profound.

10

A Glimpse into the Future

Curiouser and curiouser!

—ALICE

The industrial economy of the last century concentrated on improving economies of scale: mass-producing products to maximize the utilization of production capacity to drive down costs and maintain a consistent level of acceptable quality.

Companies in the outcome economy are no longer competing through selling cheaper and usually—but not always—better products and services. Instead, they strive to provide products and product-based services that bring meaningful, measurable results for their customers.

Smart, connected products will continue to reshape the very nature of the manufacturing enterprise, its workflow, and how it is organized, promising to create dramatic new opportunities for value creation.

But the economic impact of smart, connected products is still in its nascent stage, and the business outcomes are not easily discernible. True, the growth in the number of connected devices will continue and most likely accelerate, but the rapid increase in sheer connectivity will not always be accompanied by corresponding business results.

If the current wave of the Industrial Internet of Things is driven by ubiquitous connectivity, the next wave will be fueled by radical business transformation. It will be led by companies who are ready to change the way they do business, which will drive the evolution of their IoT offerings.

This evolution will be difficult for many companies to achieve. And there will be plenty of technology blame to go around, such as the challenges in developing and deploying embedded control software, complexities of managing product life cycles, and data security and privacy concerns.

These are no doubt important challenges that demand our attention. But they are also relatively well-defined technical problems that will be resolved by technology experts.

Realizing the promise of the Internet of Things (and meeting the lofty projections of device makers and wireless carriers) will require more than overcoming technology challenges. It will require a fundamental reorientation of the way that business strategists, technologists, and product designers work together to shape and demonstrate the value of smart, connected products.

This business evolution will require a new partnership between those who understand and advocate for the business and those who understand and integrate the technology to create that business value.

New Face of Competition

Product companies are structured to compete by building bigger and more efficient factories to turn out cheaper, safer, and (hopefully) better widgets. Competition is based on functional superiority and higher product quality. And, at the same time, built-in obsolescence is critical in order to keep the sales pipeline full and generate new product sales revenue.

Future business excellence and competitive strength will shift to what Michael Porter identifies as the "Third Wave of ICT-Driven Competition,"[50] ushering in a "new era of competition" by achieving higher levels of customer intimacy, delivering customer value, and battling over customer loyalty.

In the Industrial IoT era, forward-thinking industrial companies will take market share from their competition by aligning their business model with customer expectations and consumption preferences. Think about the Pontiac Aztek described in Chapter 7, and how GM would have benefited (twice) from having a better insight of the market.

Business and product competitiveness will take a new approach: products get better after they are bought. This improves customer satisfaction but changes business dynamics and the habit of making quick profits early in the product's life.

The Commoditization of Connectivity

While enthusiastic discussions about the valuable and profitable business outcomes afforded by the Industrial Internet of Things continue, much of the activity on the ground still focuses on device instrumentation and wireless Internet connectivity.

But, as we noted in the beginning of the previous chapter, the costs of instrumenting devices and incorporating connectivity features are dropping rapidly. Furthermore, wireless carriers and Wi-Fi hotspots are ubiquitous and inexpensive, allowing practically any device to be connected to the Internet quickly and effortlessly anywhere, anytime.

Consequently, IoT device connectivity is rapidly becoming an expected built-in capability and soon will no longer be a sufficiently differentiating feature for which customers are willing to pay extra.

Vendors of IoT connectivity hardware and those implementing Industrial IoT-based systems should realize that connectivity is rapidly becoming an expected commodity, and companies that develop market share solely based on connectivity—whether large mobile carriers or small wireless device manufacturers—are at a risk of being marginalized and losing market share to low-cost competition.

Progress Will be Frustratingly Slow

How fast is the proliferation and adoption of the Industrial Internet of Things? How soon will we be able to experience the stupendous benefits promised by the prognosticators?

Many of you who are impatient and expect this to happen overnight will be disappointed.

The ability of the industrial sectors to adopt and put the Internet of Things into practical use is dictated more by the natural cadence of industry than by the technology evolution itself. Compared to consumer electronics, the manufacturing industry moves at a turtle's pace. Industrial products take several years to get to the market and the useful lives of these machines in usually measured in decades, in contrast to the one or two years lifespan of most consumer products.

Furthermore, as we discussed earlier in the book, retrofitting manufacturing floor equipment is seldom a viable option, further slowing down the formation of large-scale Industrial Internet of Things networks.

There should be no doubt that the opportunity in Industrial IoT will cause companies to rethink product development lifecycle and accelerate the development of new products, as well as ending the life of some assets sooner than planned.

But the natural cadence of industrial manufacturing cannot be accelerated and will continue to dictate the pace of IoT adoption. The progress of the Internet of Things, especially in industrial applications will continue to be frustratingly slow. Nerveless, the opportunity is real and worth pursuing.

If the remaining useful life in shop floor machinery is too long to create a meaningful impact on the Industrial IoT in the near term, what about fast-moving items? Surely there must be industrial products with shorter lives and faster innovation cycles? Will those not benefit from being IoT-enabled?

While some consumer products can leverage the Internet of Things and provide meaningful value to consumers, in certain instances the opposite may be true. A point to consider is that products that have fast obsolescence (usually by design, so they can make room for newer products) may not have enough time to reap the benefits of IoT connectivity, and the incremental cost of additional technology may not be economically justifiable.

Chapter Takeaways

- The impact of smart, connected products is still in its nascent stage.

- Connectivity is being commoditized at a rapid rate and, in the long run, will have a diminishing differentiating value.

- Growth in Industrial IoT is hinged upon organizational transformation, as well as some industries' natural cadence of equipment updates.

- Future business excellence and competitive strength will be based on a high degree of customer intimacy, delivering customer value, and battling over customer loyalty.

Epilogue

She generally gave herself very good advice (though she very seldom followed it)...

—LEWIS CARROLL

In his epic documentary film, *Lo and Behold, Reveries of the Connected World,*[51] Director Verner Herzog says, "This is an extraordinary moment in the life of human beings." Indeed, we are only at the beginning of a truly connected world; and the implications of an always connected world are just beginning to dawn on us.

Try to imagine for a moment a world in which everyone and everything is connected.

Every product and device you use—cars, appliances, home electronics—are perfectly suited to your personal needs and wishes. They have just the features you want and aren't loaded with bells and whistles you barely understand and resent paying for. They reflect your lifestyle and personality; they are perfectly suited to you.

Not only do these machines fit your needs and personal style, they can even reconfigure themselves as your needs change, perhaps even before you know your needs are changing. Imagine that your muscle car becomes tamer when your teenage child is at the wheel.

In this world, products seem to gain new and improved functionality overnight. They are more reliable, but, when a problem does occur, they are repaired remotely. Or, when necessary, they notify you that it's time for maintenance or an upgrade.

Imagine a world in which the phrase "product ownership" has lost its meaning. Consumers and businesses no longer need to finance and insure expensive equipment. You do not have to worry about warranty terms or if the manufacturer will honor them, and you do not have to maintain the equipment because you don't actually own it. Instead, you simply buy guaranteed outcomes. It's a world in which the faint hope for customer satisfaction has turned into the guarantee of customer delight.

This is the world of hyperconnected people, businesses, and products, enabled by the Internet of Things, and it's already happening.

In the traditional, pre-digital-revolution economy, products were defined by their technical specifications, by enumerating features that product creators believed were important to customers and to which they promised to adhere.

The product promise of the past is quickly transforming into the product promise of the future, in which the ability to orchestrate, participate in, and contribute to a dynamic, interconnected, and collaborative ecosystem that continually aligns and realigns itself around worthy innovation and meaningful business outcomes, becomes the norm.

This is the emerging outcome-based economy, in which business advantage is achieved not by selling more products but by choreographing global networks of resources and information to fashion novel and highly personalized ways of bringing untapped value to customers, employees, and business partners.

That's the promise of the outcome economy. And delivering on that promise is no longer a dream that's limited to the fanciful vision of just a few. It's within the reach of every business, which will shape the way we compete and thrive in a future of nearly infinite innovation and value creation.

The question that remains is: will your organization be a leader in pursuing the promise of the future, or be a footnote in the annals of the past?

Appendix I:
Taxonomy of "Smart, Connected Things"

Glenn Lurie, President & CEO of AT&T Mobility and Consumer Operations, once said:[52]

> *Any device that is connected is smart.*

This is certainly an interesting point of view, but obviously not all "things," even if connected, are created equal. With the myriad of Industrial IoT-networked devices, each is designed to perform a different task, has varying levels of autonomy and decision-making capabilities, and carries a different role in the IoT's value chain.

An Industrial IoT-based solution is a network of diverse devices and technologies such as sensors and actuators, networking and computing devices, motors and pumps, and so forth. It is an amalgamation of different business-centric applications such as data aggregators, business analytics, and decision support systems.

The business function of the Industrial Internet of Things is based on connectivity among heterogeneous devices, each possessing different levels of built-in intelligence and autonomous operation.

Why can't all devices be simply "smart" as Mr. Lurie suggests?

First, as we discussed earlier, simpler devices that do not perform complex computational tasks are cheaper, consume less power, have a smaller physical footprint, and are less prone to failures and cyber-attacks. Admittedly, as IoT devices are becoming mainstream, some of these constraints are steadily disappearing.

It can also be argued that simple devices are less prone to hacking because of their limited command and control reach. In fact, there IoT architects that advocate not only simpler edge devices, but also, in highly vulnerable applications, the use of mixed digital and analog edge devices to create a more secure barrier between edge devices and the network hub.[53]

It is essential to understand this device heterogeneity across the value chain and how different classes of IoT devices must be able work in tandem to realize the business value of individual IoT subnetworks.

Kortuem et al[54] proposed a taxonomy model based on three canonical behavioral types: activity-aware objects, policy-aware objects, and process-aware objects. Each object has three functional and behavioral attributes:

- *Awareness* is an object's ability to understand—that is, to sense, interpret, and react to—events occurring in the physical world.
- *Representation* refers to the object's control and operation model.
- *Interaction* denotes the object's ability to communicate with other objects and with the end-user in terms of inputs, outputs, and controls.

Kortuem's model provides a good general framework to classify the portfolio Industrial Internet of Things devices. The following is a simplified IoT device taxonomy model based loosely on these principles.

Activity-Aware Devices

The basic building blocks of the Industrial IoT are single-task devices such as sensors, pumps, valves, and motors. These devices can measure and send discrete pieces of information (a sensor) or respond to a simple on/off command (a pump; a motor).

An activity-aware object "understands" the physical world in terms of event and activity streams, where each event or activity is directly related to the task the object is to perform: turn on, measure, etc.

The operating model of activity-aware devices is typically a simple linear sequence of data acquisition and processing functions, such as a time or state series. These devices measure and log data, but do not provide interactive or self-governance capabilities—they do not possess localized decision-making capabilities.

Devices in this class operate in an open loop. They have no means to gauge and communicate if the task was performed adequately. For example, a pump unit is not aware if it is delivering the specified flow and pressure. This responsibility is typically delegated to a measurement device located downstream from the pump's output.

Policy-Aware Devices

A policy-aware device is an activity-aware object with a built-in policy model. A policy-aware device can sense and interpret events and respond to them based on predefined operational and organizational policies.

Many industrial devices, even simple ones, are policy-aware devices. For example, a thermostat is commanded to maintain a certain temperature range. In other words, the thermostat has an autonomous decision-making capability to enable it to comply with the policy. An air-conditioning unit and an alarm system are other examples of policy-aware smart devices.

Having capacity for localized decision making and autonomous operation does not imply a complex digital device of the type usually associated with fancy Internet of Things scenarios. For instance, the good old round Honeywell thermostat, still found in many homes, is a very simple analog device that uses a bimetal spring and a mercury tilt switch to control temperature.

The governance model of policy-aware devices consists of application-specific policies expressed as a set of rules that operate on event and activity streams to create actions. The model provides context-sensitive information about event handling and work-activity performance, so, for example, the device can issue warnings and alerts if it's unable to comply with the policy or the operating model.

An analog thermostat cannot be programmed and commanded remotely, nor can it communicate its state, which, in essence, excludes it from being considered a smart, connected IoT device. Referring back to the three attributes of Industrial IoT objects on page 133, the representation and interaction attributes of the analog thermostat are nil. Yet, it's always illustrative to realize how many automation tasks can be accomplished using "dumb" devices.

Process-Aware Devices

A process is a collection of related activities or tasks that are sequenced in time and space to accomplish a task or a series of tasks. Process execution rules can be included for the dynamic recombination of activities to support a broader range of interrelated activities, tasks, and sub-tasks, and have greater agility and event-handling capacity.

A process-aware device is aware of and "understands" the organizational processes that it is a part of. Moreover, it is also aware of other devices in its subnetwork operating in tandem to implement the process, and can relate the occurrence of real-world activities and events of these processes to the user.

The application model of process-aware objects is built around a dynamic context-driven workflow model that defines timing and ordering of work activities. Work processes (that is, sequence and timing of activities and events) communicate with others to accomplish predefined, high-level tasks.

Examples of process-aware applications include cold chain logistics,[55] process automation and control, robots, and manufacturing execution systems (MES).[56] In addition to localized decision-making capabilities, these systems often make extensive use of business process management (BPM) engines[57] and decision-support tools to interface with process management systems and interact with human operators.

Distributed or Centralized Decision Making—Which is Better?

Internet of Things devices are able to make sophisticated process and operational decisions based on complex data aggregation and analysis, governance policies and business rules. This capacity inspires the conceptual

IoT architectures that place smart, connected devices at the edge of the IoT network.

There are some perfectly good arguments as to why more autonomous decision authority should be delegated to devices residing at the edge of the network.

For instance, moving decision-making devices closer to the industrial processes they govern improves real-time control and reduces network traffic and computational load.

On the other hand, there are also equally convincing rationales to consider the use of less sophisticated and less autonomous devices at the edge of the network.

First, simpler devices that do not need to perform complex computations are simpler and cheaper, consume less power, and are more reliable. It can also be argued that these devices are less prone to hacking because of their limited command and control reach. In fact, IoT security experts advocate not only simpler edge devices, but also, in highly vulnerable applications, the use of mixed digital and analog edge devices to create a security gap between edge devices and the network hub. [58]

Much more importantly, however, many business decisions should not and cannot be performed at the edge device level. While command and control of a single machine can be done locally and autonomously, the type of deep insight that drives predictive analytics and long-term decisions is based on multiple inputs from the broader IoT and business networks: multiple machines, multiple production lines, and multiple locales. These types of analyses and decisions should be carried out centrally.

There is no single architectural answer to the question. Arguments that computing should be pushed to the edge of the IoT network, or, conversely, be exclusively cloud-centric miss the point. The power of the Internet of Things is in a flexible decision-making architecture and the ability to move analytics and decision making as needed between edge devices, for example, for real-time control, and centralized cloud applications such as fleet optimization.

Appendix II:
Return on Investment

The question of forecasting the return on investment in the Industrial Internet of Things can be tricky. Corporate executives nowadays are applying greater investment scrutiny than ever before and do not approve of investments whose payback period does not appear fast and promising enough. And when project proponents and planners try to be more optimistic (and less realistic) about how long it would take to recover the investment, they are accused of donning rose-colored glasses.

Indeed, demonstrating a credible return on investment (ROI) model in IoT does seem like a significant and somewhat risky proposition: you need to design special product features, create the network infrastructure, worry about data security, engage in new business models, and so on. You will need to recruit and train new personnel. The time to revenue and positive cashflow seems to get farther and farther with every step.

When you analyze the investment using traditional financial tools, you may not like the results. In all likelihood, management won't like them either.

But there is an alternative approach.

A well-established concept in economics called *real options valuation*[59] defines certain investments as an instrument that grants the buyer an option— but not the obligation—to undertake certain future business initiatives.

Professor Robert Fichman of Boston College published several articles[60] in which he describes a model of the determinants of option value associated with investments in innovative ICT platforms. The model addresses a central question: When should an organization should invest in an emerging technology, and how to assess the risks and upsides of that investment.

Under a real options investment strategy, the investment in the infrastructure of the

Internet of Things is only a means to an end— a platform upon which future revenue‑generating products and services may be built.

As such, the IOT platform investment is not required to have any ROI, because, in itself— i.e., without the additional services that drive customer business outcome—it has no, or very small, intrinsic value. Obviously, subsequent investments in products, people, and business networks should be able to undergo due diligence and financial scrutiny.

Endnotes

[1] https://www.renfe.com/EN/empresa/index.html

[2] https://en.wikipedia.org/wiki/Theodore_Levitt

[3] https://www.rolls-royce.com/products-and-services/civil-aerospace/services/services-catalogue/totalcare.aspx

[4] http://www.inc.com/thomas-koulopoulos/5-of-the-biggest-trends-for-2016-that-you-probably-haven-t-even-heard-of.html

[5] https://en.wikipedia.org/wiki/Theodore_Paraskevakos

[6] http://www.networkcomputing.com/networking/internet-things-ip-address-needs/1170065007

[7] https://en.wikipedia.org/wiki/Cloud_computing

[8] https://en.wikipedia.org/wiki/Internet_of_Things. Retrieved April 25, 2016.

[9] https://www.onstar.com

[10] http://autoweek.com/article/car-news/improving-quality-onstar

[11] http://www.mobileye.com/en-us

[12] It is impossible to define an exact chronology of events and milestones, but Chapter Two in *The World is Flat* by Thomas Freidman (www.amazon.com/The-World-Is-Flat-Twenty-first/dp/0374292884) provides a good background reading.

[13] http://www.evineyardapp.com/

[14] https://www.libelium.com

[15] https://www.dolphin-engineering.ch

[16] https://www.konecranes.com

[17] https://www.amazon.com/Wisdom-Crowds-James-Surowiecki/dp/0385721706

[18] https://standards.ieee.org/findstds/standard/wired_and_wireless_communications.html

[19] www.amazon.com/The-Wisdom-Crowds-James-Surowiecki/dp/0385721706 https://openwsn.atlassian.net/wiki/display/OW/Home

[20] https://www.iatn.net

[21] https://www.ge.com/ar2015/letter

[22] https://en.wikipedia.org/wiki/William_Gibson

[23] http://www.amazon.com/Liquid-Enterprise-transforming-business-leadership/dp/1908984619

[24] https://www.finfacts.ie/irishfinancenews/article_1028082.shtml. Retrieved April 27, 2016.

[25] https://www.ifm.eng.cam.ac.uk/research/dstools/innovation-funnel/

[26] https://en.wikipedia.org/wiki/Phase-gate_model

[27] https://www.roadandtrack.com/car-culture/a6357/bob-lutz-tells-the-inside-story-of-the-pontiac-aztek-debacle/ Retrieved April 27, 2016.

[28] https://www.edmunds.com/about/press/dodge-magnum-scores-highest-with-millennials-on-used-car-market-says-edmundscom.html. Retrieved April 27, 2016.

[29] http://www.amc.com/shows/breaking-bad

[30] http://adage.com/article/advertising/big-spenders-facts-stats-top-200-u-s-advertisers/299270/. Retrieved May 3, 2016

[31] https://www.roadandtrack.com/car-culture/a6357/bob-lutz-tells-the-inside-story-of-the-pontiac-aztek-debacle/ Retrieved April 27, 2016.

[32] https://www.bsquare.com/case-study/coca-cola-freestyle/

[33] https://en.wikipedia.org/wiki/Reliability-centered_maintenance

[34] https://www.tivall.co.uk/content.asp?id=14

[35] https://www.augury.com/

[36] https://www.ge.com/digital/products/smartsignal

[37] http://www.siemens.com/digitalization/digital-services.html

[38] While the Digitization vs. Digitalization debate is far from being settled, we use digitalization here to mean "the adoption or increase in use of digital or computer technology by an organization, industry, country, etc." http://culturedigitally.org/2014/09/digitalization-and-digitization/

[39] http://www.sciencedirect.com/science/article/pii/S0957417497000183

[40] https://en.wikipedia.org/wiki/Edward_Feigenbaum

[41] https://www.gartner.com/doc/2930917/predicts--step-change-industrialization (restricted access)

[42] https://en.wikipedia.org/wiki/Machine_learning

[43] https://en.wikipedia.org/wiki/Artificial_neural_network

[44] https://en.wikipedia.org/wiki/Brute-force_search

[45] http://www.amazon.com/Real-Time-Enterprise-Competing-Revolutionary-Business/dp/0929652304

[46] http://www.amazon.com/Competitive-Advantage-Creating-Sustaining-Performance/dp/0684841460

[47] How Smart, Connected Products Are Transforming Companies, Harvard Business Review October 2015

[48] MIT Technology Review, July-August 2014

[49] *Technology, Management and Society*
http://books.google.com/books?id=FC8sBgAAQBAJ&
vq

[50] How Smart, Connected Products Are Transforming
Competition, Harvard Business Review November
2014

[51] http://www.imdb.com/title/tt5275828/

[52] https://www.scribd.com/doc/207595339/The-Silent-
Intelligence-Daniel-Kellmereit

[53] http://www.bloomberg.com/news/articles/2016-03-
10/cybersecurity-the-best-insurance-may-be-analog

[54] Kortuem, G.; Kawsar, F.; Fitton, D.; Sundramoorthy,
V. "Smart Objects as Building Blocks for the Internet
of things" *IEEE Internet Computing* Volume 14,
Issue 1

[55] https://en.wikipedia.org/wiki/Cold_chain

[56] https://en.wikipedia.org/wiki/Manufacturing_
execution_system

[57] https://en.wikipedia.org/wiki/Business_process_
management

[58] https://www.bloomberg.com/news/articles/2016-03-
10/cybersecurity-the-best-insurance-may-be-analog

[59] https://en.wikipedia.org/wiki/Real_options_valuation

[60] http://pubsonline.informs.org/doi/abs/10.1287/
isre.1040.0021

76374667R00092

Made in the USA
Columbia, SC
07 September 2017